Retreats

Retreats

HANDMADE HIDEAWAYS TO REFRESH THE SPIRIT

G. Lawson Drinkard, III

GIBBS·SMITH
PUBLISHER

SAIT LAKE CITY

First edition
00 99 98 97   5 4 3 2 1

This is a Peregrine Smith Book, published by
Gibbs Smith, Publisher
P.O. Box 667
Layton, Utah 84041
Toll-free (1-800) 748-5439 *orders only*

Design by J. Scott Knudsen, Park City, Utah
Printed in Hong Kong
Illustratons by Damian Farrell, Damian Farrell Design
Group, Ann Arbor, Michigan

The information in this book is accurate to the best of
our knowledge. Its purpose is to help the reader do some
creative thinking regarding the idea of personal retreat
and what criteria are important to the individual. None of
the information is intended to show the reader how to
build or create anything, only to heighten the reader's
imagination as to what might be possible. The author and
publisher encourage anyone considering building a retreat
to seek professional advice and guidance. Recommended
reading and resources are provided for informational
purposes. The author and publisher take no responsibility
for their content or performance.

Library of Congress Cataloging-in-Publication Data
Retreats : handmade hideaways to refresh the spirit / by
G. Lawson Drinkard, III. p.   cm.
ISBN 0-87905-798-X
    1. Second homes—Design and construction—
Amateurs' manuals. 2. House construction—Amateurs'
manuals. I. Title.
TH4835.D75   1997
690'.837—dc21   97-1829
                                        CIP

To my father and mother,
who taught me to believe
that I could be whatever
I wanted to be, and that
I could accomplish whatever
I set my mind to.

CONTENTS

ACKNOWLEDGMENTS 9

To Begin With
10

Getting Started
14

Multiple Choices
24

PROFILES—PEOPLE AND PLACES 42

Last Contact
42

Canyon Tree House
52

An Architect's Retreat
58

Sod-roofed Sanctuary
66

Tar Paper
Shack
74

The Executive
Suite
120

Tipi by
the River
80

Main Street
Retreat
126

Wilson
Wyoming
Women
86

Winter
Retreats
134

The Houses
that Baird
Built
100

RETREATS IN
WAITING
142

Musings
on Zuni
110

REFERENCES AND RESOURCES 152

I have learned to be content with whatever I have.

PHILIPPIANS 4:11

ONE CAN'T DO a project like this book alone. It takes a community of mentors, friends, and colleagues. I've been blessed by such a group, and I owe heartfelt thanks and a substantial debt of gratitude to many. Names are important. At the risk of an oversight, the following have helped, influenced, nurtured, and cared for me all along the way.

Thanks . . .

to Carol Troxell for her assistance in locating research materials, for feeding my eclectic reading habits, and for treating me all along like a real author.

to Sue Simpson for connecting me with delightful people and places, and for introducing me to art that brings me joy.

to Jon Golden for a keen eye, fine photographs, and a willingness to travel economically.

to Bob Vickery for seeing some potential way back when and encouraging me to express it.

to Mary Ann Elwood for her love of language and her gentle reminders that the grammar police are always active.

to Don McMillan for good questions and helping me find the path.

to Terry Baird, who said no so I could say yes

and who hauled us all over the hills for photographs and conversation.

to Dayton Duncan, whose writings caused me to think about some new directions.

to Arch and Jane Wagner, who gave me the chance to design my first log cabin.

to Dawna Markova, who helped me see how I could actually finish and volunteered to be my book-birthing midwife.

to my editor, Madge Baird, whose guidance, enthusiasm, encouragement, and tireless effort helped transform this book from an idea to a reality.

to Jeane and Steve Aller for translating the language of our adopted state, for making their ranch our second home, and for their unfaltering friendship and support.

to Trish and Ron Higgins, Beth and Jay Sanderford, and Marci and Charlie Mason, who listened, asked, comforted, believed, cared, and occasionally offered a gentle kick in the seat of the pants.

and finally, to my wife, Suzanne, and daughter, Sarah, who lived with me every day of the way, provided oceans full of support, and are the loves of my life.

LAWSON DRINKARD
March 1997

A retreat on the West
Boulder River near
McLeod, Montana, built
almost entirely of sal-
vaged and reclaimed
materials, sits in the
landscape as if it has
been there for fifty years.

TO BEGIN WITH . . .

With the possible exception of the equator,
everything begins somewhere.

PETER FLEMING

(from *One's Company,* 1934)

I CAN JUST BARELY conjure up an image of the first retreat I remember, which I built when I was around eight years old with my then best friend, Pete Obenschain, and his pesky little brother, Tommy. From somewhere in our Virginia small-town neighborhood, we salvaged enough barely rotting planks to build a wooden box that was just big enough to hold three or four small boys squeezed tightly together, dressed in whatever costumes represented our dreams on that particular day. In our fantasy world, this rickety wooden box was a sacred place, a place where pacts were made, plans were hatched, and from which neighborhood assaults were launched. It was a private place, a hands-off place, a place where moms were off limits and girls didn't dare to enter. In due time, that "clubhouse" ran its course, and those same boards became a new hideout—a tree house spread across the well-used boughs of Mrs. McGreggor's mulberry tree. The Swiss Family Robinson, Blackbeard the pirate, and General Robert E. Lee all played there at one time or another.

My childhood was filled with adventures in small spaces, and those moments have stuck like pine pitch to the deep recesses of my psyche. My cousin Mary Sue and I built hideaway spaces in my grandmother's backyard with old quilts hung over a framework of my grandfather's green Adirondack chairs. Dozens of summer hours were whiled away as our imaginations let us become the king and queen of most anywhere in the universe. The first time my family went camping, I lived for a week in a mustard-brown canvas wall tent at the base of a soapstone cliff in the Blue Ridge Mountains of Virginia. For high-style entertainment, my Uncle Paul carved small trinkets for all of the cousins out of the soft cliff rock.

In 1962 I spent some howling stormy nights and sweltering hot days at Hatteras Island on the Outer Banks of North Carolina in the "Chartreuse Caboose"—a plywood and fiberglass "tent trailer," homebuilt by my father before pop-up campers became commercially available and popular. I traveled to the 1964 New York World's Fair in a 1952 Cadillac hearse that my dad and Uncle Roy had converted into a homemade mobile vacation home, long before the recreational-vehicle craze struck the highways and campgrounds of America. I had my first view of the St. Lawrence Seaway through its windshield and made my first international border crossing in the double-bed bunk that hovered above the cab. Small, inti-

mate, inexpensive by necessity, and made by caring hands, these places left a powerful impression on my mind, my heart, and indeed on my whole being.

My high school and college years were filled with retreat-like adventures and places. Winter hunting trips with my father included subzero-degree nights spent in an old chicken coop, anticipating predawn forays into the woods in pursuit of whitetail deer and wild turkeys. Spring weekends were often passed trout fishing and skinny-dipping in the river running next to Tom Beam's family "camp" in the mountains of western Virginia. Summers were spent living in a virtual shack of a dormitory while working at a Presbyterian church camp and retreat center. Spare moments were frequently organized into adventures, crawling around the 54-degree limestone wombs of the caverns and caves of Virginia and West Virginia. And then there was the college-town apartment in a windowless basement that was transformed into a palace with a few cheap posters, Barney the SPCA beagle, chianti bottles with candles, and a patchwork rug made of carpet remnants glued to an old canvas tarp. Sights, sounds, and smells attached to youthful experiences of wonder, joy, learning, and love—these simple but potent impressions have brought me full circle.

After a formal education in architecture at

the University of Virginia and several years of apprenticeship in a small firm, I found myself part owner of a start-up architecture firm in Charlottesville, Virginia. The next fifteen years were invested with wonderful colleagues in inventing, starting, learning, growing, changing, and developing a successful business. Like many entrepreneurs, we focused our business efforts on growth—bigger buildings, larger commissions, numbers of design awards, additional staff, higher profits, and more clients—which always seemed to leave less time for reading, learning, reflecting, having dialogue, and living with quality. It was a heady and frequently satisfying time but not without an occasional twitch of questioning and discontent.

There has always existed for me a search for meaning—for that which was calling me forward. Sometimes it has been on an unconscious level that my ship has been tugged forward on an erratic course to some unidentified island in the ocean of life. At other times I have worked consciously with colleagues to try to identify our personal callings and how those connected to our collective "vision" for the business. The answers weren't usually complete, were never easy, and only came in small chunks at a time after much thought and reflection.

Somewhere along the way, a good friend reintroduced me to fly-fishing for trout after a hiatus of nearly twenty years. Soon I began to realize that, for me, this was a retreat-like activity. Trout fishing usually takes place in areas of intense physical beauty, far away from the daily rigors of the phone and fax machine; and to be successful at it, one must clear the mind and focus on the stream, the bugs, the wind, the currents, and the fish. I began to reconnect to the outdoors, to nature, to old friends, and to my roots.

Eventually these disparate but connected activities began to lead me on a quest to discover the answers to the following question: Where do people go and what do they do when they want to get away from it all, to reflect, to question, to rest their mind and refresh their spirit, to lose themselves in order to find themselves again?

At first my investigations were mostly about the physical places of retreat—about the rooms, spaces, buildings, or shelters set aside to afford a person seclusion, privacy, peace, quiet, and solitude. These places could be described with such words as refuge, haven, hideout, and sanctuary. They take the form of cabins, cottages, caves, trailers, tents, and shacks. I asked the questions an architect might ask: What kind of structure makes a good retreat? How is it built? What does it look like? What are the essential design considerations? How long does it take? How much does it cost? Where can I find these retreats?

While on this voyage of discovery, however, I learned that people and place are inextricably tied together. Retreat is as much about the person as it is about the place where it occurs. Along the research road, I had the good fortune to meet and interview dozens of fascinating people who were searching for, or had found, the essence of retreat for themselves. Then the questions began to change: Why would you do this? What are the key ingredients, the indispensable properties, the crucial elements? What makes it work for you? What are the benefits? What advice might you have for others? How do you derive meaning from this experience?

So, it is through these images of retreats and these voices of retreat builders that I hope to convey some practical and useful information, to answer some of these questions, and most importantly, to raise some additional questions for your consideration.

For me, retreat is not a location; it is a state of mind. It is not a destination but rather a journey. It is not a moment in time but a lifetime pursuit. If you decide to make a place for your body's relaxation and your spirit's refreshment, I wish you many moments of inspiration, rest, creativity, and joy. And foremost, enjoy the expedition!

GETTING STARTED

Go confidently in the direction of your dreams! Live the life you've imagined. As you simplify your life, the laws of the universe will be simpler.

HENRY DAVID THOREAU

WHERE DOES ONE begin when setting out to create a personal retreat space? With a dream? With a site? With a budget? With a set of drawings? With an existing structure or a pile of old materials? *Starting,* of course, is a relative term. Starting could assume that you have been musing about having such a place for long enough that the time has come to make it a reality. Beginning could also be defined as commencing a more intensified dreaming effort. Unlike some other projects, starting at the beginning is not necessarily required, expected, or even the best way. If you are one of those people who absolutely has to start at the beginning, then go ahead and do so. If you just want to jump in the middle and work outward, go for it! Start wherever your spirit moves you.

No matter where you choose to begin, there are two aspects that will eventually need to be confronted. They are purpose or potential use, and place. Practical considerations, such as types of structures, new versus rehabilitated or adapted, and some specific features will be covered in a later chapter.

PURPOSE AND POTENTIAL USES

Perhaps the broad answer as to the question of purpose for a retreat seems blatantly obvious. "I just need a place to get away!" For many people there seems to be a component of the human spirit that demands just that—a place of one's own to relax, rest, recharge, and center. If that message is calling you forward, by all means, try to find a way to act on this intuition.

In today's society most adults lead lives full of complexity, with a multitude of demands on time and resources. In a search for a simpler way—or some simpler time along the way—it may be helpful to take some time to examine the specific purpose for your own personal retreat. Will it be activity-related, vocation-related, or avocation-related? Will it include hunting, skiing, fishing, painting, potting, or writing? Should it be solitary or inclusive of others? For some, examining questions such as these is just too much work and may inhibit getting started. For others, this kind of probing leads to a deeper understanding of self, and thus begins to capture one of the key ingredients of retreat—questioning one's self and evaluating the essence of one's life.

One can engage in this kind of introspection while planning a retreat or after creating one. If you choose to follow this path, an activity like the following one might get you started:

Write some lists of aspects of a retreat, or of retreating, that are meaningful to you. Large easel pads work well for this activity so your pages can be hung on the wall for reference as you are going along.

Consider questions like these:

- For you, what is important about the idea of retreat?
- What are your special dreams and aspirations for this place?
- What will this retreat make possible for you?
- What will make it possible to have your retreat?
- How will you use your retreat?
- When will you use this place?
- Why will you use your retreat?
- Who will use this place?
- What might you need, or what are you willing to give up to have a physical place for retreat?
- What might you need to give up to have time to retreat?
- For you, what is essential about this retreat?
- For you, what is not essential about this retreat?

These questions will probably lead to more. Keep good notes or perhaps start a journal. Making sure your retreat meets the criteria you will have defined will assure your greater enjoyment of it.

PLACE

The choice of place for a retreat may be the most important and difficult task for the aspiring builder. Issues to be considered when choosing a place include cost of land, zoning, natural characteristics, and distance from your permanent residence. All of these issues affect other practical ones, such as:

- How long might it take to build?
- How easy (or difficult, or costly) will it be to build?
- How often can the retreat be used?
- What will be the "hassle" factor in getting it built?

For some, place doesn't seem to matter at all. One place is as good as another. For others, place is everything. The deliberation about where to create your retreat will draw out many clues as to what is meaningful to you about being there. Some yearn for the mountains, some for the desert, and some for the sea. Some want total seclusion and some want a sense of community. Some want snow and some want eternal spring. Many people have fond childhood memories of riverside camps, of summers on grandma and grandpa's farm, or of primitive mountain cabins. These deep impressions have shaped, or will shape, the place and style of their own retreats.

Your place can be as close as your backyard, a corner of your pasture, or even the end of your attic or basement. It can be as far away as you are willing to travel to get away and cleanse your spirit.

Let's consider some of the factors of place:

Land Costs

Land costs can run from nothing, if you already own some property, to many thousands of dollars if you don't. Some realtors are fond of saying about land that "they are not making any more of it," and finding a choice spot for the right price is becoming more and more challenging. Compared to the other expenses associated with a relatively small and simple retreat, land costs could end up being ten or even a hundred times the cost of the structure itself.

For most, cost is—or should be—a consideration. Before sacrificing your dream for an idyllic retreat place because land is too expensive, step back and try to be creative. A visit with a local farmer, rancher, builder, attorney, or building official might reveal a leftover, unusual, or topographically difficult piece of property that might be perfect for an unorthodox structure. Sometimes pieces of property are sold for back taxes, so a careful inspection of the legal notices in the local newspaper combined with a creative spirit can produce remarkable results for little money expended. Long-term land leases might be an option, especially if you decide to build a simple

and inexpensive, disposable, or mobile retreat— when the lease is up, either move it or leave it!

A tiny piece of property, properly situated, can seem much larger than it actually is. Our personal family retreat is located on a relatively narrow strip of land by a river, but on the other side of that river is a steep mountainside and vast forest owned by the United States of America and managed by the Forest Service. The views are expansive and unobstructed and have the practical effect of increasing the size of our property considerably.

Zoning and Building Codes

Almost but not every county and city in America is now governed by some sort of building code and land-use zoning. There are still a few areas without zoning, but as people continue to seek out and migrate to these areas, the people who govern and care about these places must all face the appropriate land-use questions someday.

Building codes are intended to insure safe and healthy structures, and zoning ordinances are intended to guide land development and to assure compatible uses of various pieces of property. Depending upon your perspective, these laws are designed for community and personal protection or they interfere with individual rights. No matter how you may feel about them, zoning and building codes are here to stay and need to be a part of your planning process. I know of a multistory condominium project on the Outer Banks of North Carolina where the top floors of several new buildings had to be removed because the owners did not pay attention to, or believe in, the height limitations in the zoning laws.

In some areas, zoning stipulations are very strictly enforced, and in other places, even though they exist, they are not imposed at all. As you consider a place for your retreat structure, you will want to gain a working knowledge of the local land-use ordinances as well as an

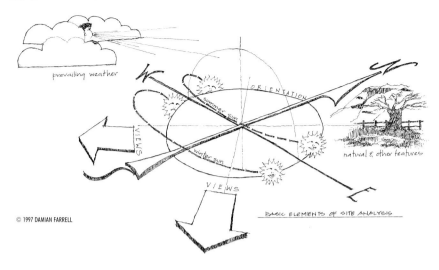

© 1997 DAMIAN FARRELL

understanding of how they are enforced and who enforces them. A visit to the local building official's office will answer the basic questions. Conversations with local contractors, building suppliers, real-estate agents, or land-use attorneys can provide more useful information. Some sites will be harder to gain approval for than others, and it is always a good idea to get a feel in advance for how much effort will be required. Sites that have tough, seemingly impossible zoning restrictions for some kinds of uses may present an opportunity to buy an inexpensive piece of land for a creative retreat situation.

Usually, building officials have a fairly easy time interpreting zoning ordinances and building codes when what you want to build is a routine permanent structure such as a small cabin, house, or barn. When things don't fit the normal mold, or if they are not spelled out in a zoning ordinance, much more is left to the discretion of the local administrator. Temporary or mobile structures such as wall tents, tipis, yurts, and travel trailers may not come under the jurisdiction of a local zoning ordinance at all. But what if they are, or become, permanent structures? How will the building official interpret things if you decide to build a tree house

and "tree house" is not defined in the ordinance? Any structure on any site in any locality will present the possibility of different code and zoning issues and different interpretations by the local building officials. With patience and perseverance, most site and code obstacles can usually be worked out. One can adopt a "what they don't know won't hurt them" attitude, but skipping steps in a local approval process could result in difficulties in the future.

Natural Characteristics

Your potential site should be evaluated for all of the same natural characteristics that builders have been looking at over the centuries when considering a dwelling. They include sun and shade, prevailing winds, topography, drainage, access to water, security, views (to and from), and locations for other appurtenances you may eventually want on the site (outhouse, sauna, woodshed, guest quarters, barn, hot tub, etc.).

Orientation

The orientation of your retreat structure on the land with respect to the sun and prevailing winds will largely determine how cool it is in the summer and how warm it is in the winter, as well as the costs associated with maintaining a

This view, framed by the window, hangs like a painting in Bill Schenck's home.

desired temperature. Prevailing summer breezes can be used for natural cooling, and prevailing winter winds need to be anticipated to minimize heat loss. Local residents are the best source of knowledge about these predictable winds, or you can contact local or national weather officials.

The sun rises and sets in a completely predictable path—it has for years! Sun intensity, angles, directions, and rising and setting times vary, depending on season and geographic location. The local library reference desk can help locate that information for your specific area. If you like the morning sun in your sleeping room or late afternoon sun on an outdoor deck, make sure the site you have chosen will allow for these orientations. With proper attention to location of building and windows, passive solar energy can help to heat almost any structure. By anticipating higher summer sun angles, existing trees can be used for effective solar screening.

Views

View may be the highest-ranking reason for anyone who chooses a retreat site. Each individual knows what causes any view to be the perfect one for them. Views, however, are not always the way they first appear. Make sure your view is tested from the actual place you will be standing or sitting when your retreat is in place. How high will the finished floor be? How big will the windows be? Don't choose a site for the perfect view and then not be able to see it from your finished retreat. Go to the trouble of hauling a folding chair or ladder and placing it in the exact location you anticipate sitting to watch the sunset, and see how it looks, how it feels, and if it really works for you. I once had a client who engaged a surveyor to calculate the exact angles and sight lines from a specific finished floor elevation to the mountain peaks beyond. He wanted to be sure that "what you see is what you get."

Also, think about the range of views you want to capture. By focusing entirely on a long-range

view of distant mountain peaks, you might miss a better mid-range view of a grassy hillside or a short-range view of a beautiful grove of aspen or maple trees. These views can be framed, like photographs, by various architectural elements such as doorways, windows, and porch railings. Don't forget the changing seasons. A view you have in the winter may be totally obstructed by leafy trees in the summer.

When choosing your retreat site for a view, you should also consider not only the view *from* your retreat but the view *of* your retreat. There is nothing more offensive to your neighbors than a building stuck on the highest possible point of land for everyone within miles to have to look at whether they want to or not.

The nature of a retreat for some is the act of seclusion. Think about how your retreat might be totally hidden from view. This can pay off both for privacy when you are there and for security when you are not.

Topography

Topography can be a key factor in a site selection. The building choices one has will be affected by such things as slope, trees, rocks, water, drainage, and access. All of these factors

Outstanding results may be gained by testing a view. Arch Wagner, the owner of this house, built a platform on the site prior to construction in order to set floor heights, window sizes, furniture placement, and deck locations to capture the maximum benefits of his outstanding view opportunities.

should be studied as to the relative problems and opportunities presented by each and their relationship to each other. They all will have some effect on the overall project cost—additive or subtractive. For example, a steeply sloped site is generally more difficult to build on and has fewer construction-type options, but it usually offers more dramatic design opportunities and sometimes economies associated with stacking spaces.

A site strewn with boulders usually has subsurface rock, which can present foundation and septic field challenges but can offer building material (stone walls, fireplaces, etc.) and interesting focal points for exterior spaces. Loose rocks on steep slopes can present slide dangers, particularly in areas that have significant freeze-thaw cycles.

Trees can hide a cabin, provide shade, and bestow constantly changing short-range views, but they can also shed dead limbs or uproot and come crashing down from the effects of wind or ice storms. Over time, excessive shade is not good for buildings. The lack of light and air promotes mildew, decay, and in some areas termites. Depending on the type of tree and the density of the forest, grasses, or underbrush, fire hazards should be taken into account.

Drainage considerations should be examined in two areas—surface-water drainage and septic percolation (absorption). Both affect the viability of building and the value of a potential site.

Care should be taken not to build in a low-lying area that will collect and hold moisture or in a natural swale that may direct volumes of runoff onto or into your new retreat. Constant dampness around the base of a building can promote mold, mildew, and rotting timbers. In order to avoid these problems, sites can be built up with fill dirt or gravel. Water diversion devices such as earth berms, walls, and underground drainage systems can be added. All of these landscape alterations will add effort and expense to your retreat project; therefore, it is desirable to select a site that avoids their necessity.

If you intend to install a septic tank and drain field, the site will need to meet the physical conditions that will allow it to operate correctly. An underground septic tank, distribution box, and absorption field will be required for normal installations. The ground must percolate, or have the proper absorption, for the controlled seepage of liquid effluent from the tank. Requirements vary from jurisdiction to jurisdiction, but even in remote areas, these systems are usually carefully regulated by governmental authorities for reasons of maintaining water quality and other health-related issues. A local building official or septic-system installer can provide the information and standards you need. If the land doesn't percolate or if it is impractical to install such a system, other options are available. An excellent resource for detailed information on retreat septic systems, alternative toilets, and drinking water systems is *Cottage Water Systems* by Max Burns.

Access to water is an imperative quality for any site that will be occupied any longer than can be supplied by what you are willing to carry in on your back or haul in a truck. Water weighs 8⅓ pounds per gallon, so the limitations are obvious! Though free-flowing streams are a wonderful natural quality for any retreat site, there are virtually none left in America that are safe for providing drinking water without some form of treatment. If your site has a spring, it might be wise to test the water quality for potability before purchasing the land. If you intend to rely on a cistern, check the annual rainfall rates, and if you intend to bore, drill, or dig a well, check with the locals to determine an average depth you can expect to probe before reaching this necessary elixir. Remember, any septic system or privy must be *at a lower elevation* than your source of water and at least 100 feet away. Again, local regulations may vary, so check first.

Site access is one of the most significant impacts of land topography. Roads are expensive—in the range of $10–$20 a running foot,

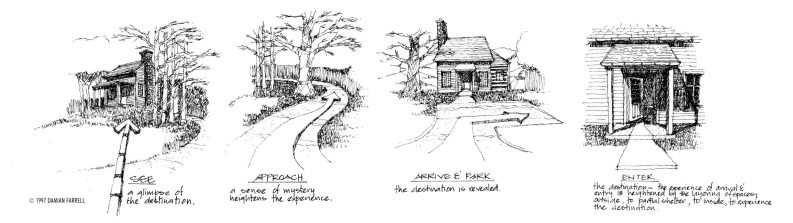

SEE
a glimpse of
the destination.

© 1997 DAMIAN FARRELL

APPROACH
a sense of mystery
heightens the experience.

ARRIVE & PARK.
the destination is revealed.

ENTER.
the destination~ the experience of arrival &
entry is heightened by the layering of spaces;
outside, to partial shelter, to inside, to experience
the destination.

and the steeper they are, the more costly they get and the harder they are to navigate. Any grade higher than 14 percent (1 foot of elevation rise for every 7 feet of horizontal run) almost makes four-wheel drive a necessity. Other considerations include width, configuration, subsurface conditions, grades, drainage, surfacing, and arrival sequence. A road needs to be wide enough to accommodate the traffic it will bear, including construction vehicles (don't forget the concrete truck!). Subsurface soil conditions must be sufficient to support a road, or stronger material must be added. Avoiding standing puddles and ponds is a must to keep a road from turning into an eventual mud bog. Surfaces can range from dirt to gravel, asphalt, or concrete, all with monetary consequences. After you arrive, there needs to be a place to park the car—and turn it around. I am familiar with one small cabin hanging from the side of a mountain with a road so steep and parking so precarious that the owner has to put blocks under the wheels of his truck in case the brakes fail, and has to back several hundred yards down his driveway because there is no place to turn around. It works for him, but it wouldn't suit most people.

Another topographical access issue has to do with getting materials to the site for construction. If you choose a backcountry site with no vehicular access, you must consider how that changes the choices you make for construction

methods and materials selection. These days, nothing is impossible when it comes to construction as long as one is willing to pay. On a trip over the Beartooth Highway northeast of Cody, Wyoming, I observed a helicopter delivering material to a construction site. This shipping method is probably out of reach for the average weekend retreat builder.

An old landscape-planning adage promotes this sequence when designing the roadway to any site—See, Approach, Arrive, Park, Enter. *See* the entry or have a glimpse of the final destination; design an interesting and safe *Approach* with some mystery and delight; when you are there, make sure there is a feeling of *Arrival;* have a convenient and accessible place to *Park* (and turn around); and make sure this allows a gracious pedestrian *Entry* sequence to your retreat. Keeping each of these factors in order and in mind when examining a piece of property or laying out your road will lead to a more aesthetically appealing and well-suited final product.

The topography of any site can be adjusted to some degree. If it is done by hand, it is slow going and just plain hard work. If done by machine, it is usually quite expensive and, unless great care is exercised, can scar the natural landscape irreparably. Any hill can be made flat with a big enough bulldozer, but is that what creating a sensitive retreat is all

about? Careful attention in advance to all of the details and potential effects of any site's topography is important to a successful retreat-building experience.

Distance

Given today's mobile society, retreats can be, and are, located just about anywhere. Though it is perfectly obvious that the farther away one's retreat is, the harder (and probably more expensive) it is to get to, there are still useful questions to be asked when considering distance.

- For you, is retreat a once- or twice-a-year "event" or do you require weekly doses?
- For you, is the act of traveling (flying, driving, riding the train) a part of the retreat experience or is it a burden that causes stress?
- If you choose a faraway location for your retreat, what will be your plan for looking after the place when you are not there?
- Are there special events or activities that for you can only be enjoyed in a specific location?
- Do you want your friends to visit often, occasionally, or not at all?
- Is close by actually far enough away to retreat from daily activities, phone, fax, pager, and drop-in visitors?
- What is the middle ground?

These questions and others like them will help the aspiring retreat maker to continue to ask the important questions of why and how and where. Resist the temptation to make these decisions impulsively, but rather make this deliberation part of your preparation for getting the most out of your retreat experience.

PHOTO © PACIFIC YURTS

A yurt only requires a flat spot as large as its own diameter. This one becomes a fishing cabin perched high above a lake.

SITE-SELECTION CHECKLIST

The following list may be a helpful reference for the potential retreat purchaser or builder:

ZONING AND LEGAL ISSUES

- Is the property zoned? If so, how?
- What zoning restrictions exist for this specific piece of property?
- Is there a local building code, and does it apply?
- Are there any deed restrictions?
- What are the yearly taxes?
- Is the property in the flood plain or a wetlands area?
- Are there deeded riparian rights or mineral rights?
- Are the property lines correctly defined?
- Are there existing rights-of-way across the land?
- Is a title search necessary?

NATURAL CHARACTERISTICS

- What is the direction of the prevailing winds or breezes?
- What are the views *from* your retreat—long-range, mid-range, short-range?
- What will be the views *of* your retreat from adjacent properties?
- How does the sunlight move across the property in each season?
- What is the topography and slope of the property?
- Are there trees and natural formations that need to be considered?

- Does the soil percolate?
- Is there evidence of subsurface stone?
- Is there a potable water source?
- What is the local success rate for drilling, digging, or boring a well?
- Does the site drain properly?
- Where will the road or driveway go, and what will be the necessary grades?
- Can building materials be delivered?

UTILITIES

- Is electricity available?
- Is telephone service available? Do you want it?
- Is natural or bottled gas available?
- Is "city" water available?
- Is sewage disposal available?
- Is there a handy source for firewood?

LOCATION

- How far away is your permanent home?
- How far away from the site are the various services you deem necessary (grocery store, medical facility, library, post office, bank, church)?
- How far away are the various building trades and suppliers (concrete, lumber, plumbing, electrical, road grading, septic system)?
- How far away is the nearest fire department (this will affect your property insurance rates)?
- How close are the nearest neighbors? How close do you want them to be?
- Is there a local bar?

By no means should this be considered a definitive list of questions, but it should get you started and help to generate some more.

This traditional cabin on the Boulder River Ranch is built with a low ceiling, making the space cozy, intimate, and easier to heat.

MULTIPLE CHOICES

Imagination is more important than knowledge.

ALBERT EINSTEIN

WHEN ONE CONSIDERS the basics of building a retreat, there are many different opportunities and practical alternatives to mull. You might have noticed a theme by now. Weighing various choices and possibilities is an exercise that will not only induce a more complete opus but will also help to draw you into the essence of the retreat experience.

From a practical point of view, there are at least four approaches to structures that could be used to build a retreat. They are new structures, adapted structures, salvaged structures, and portable structures. There is not necessarily a clear distinction between these four categories. One could have a new portable structure, or a salvaged structure that is portable or adapted. New is new if it's new for you. You get the picture. I'm not going to try to put every example and type in a clear category, but rather show them as they seem to make the best sense and where they are likely to be most useful to the reader.

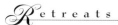

NEW STRUCTURES

This building type can generally be defined as a cabin or cottage built from scratch, from the ground up, with new materials. It can be built from a precut kit or can be custom-designed and built from individually purchased parts. It may use traditional building methods and technology such as logs, masonry, or wood frame, or it may explore alternative techniques such as straw-bale or rammed-earth construction. There are literally hundreds of building forms and technologies that could be looked at as new construction. This section will only touch on a few.

Log Construction

Log buildings have been used for shelter by people around the globe and were one of the prevalent forms of shelter for early immigrants to America. For them, it was a practical matter of needing to clear land for crops, which made trees abundant as a construction material. The log cabin has become an American symbol for a vacation retreat. Though the essential natural resource is more and more limited, the log-building industry churns along, and thousands of log houses are built every year—from diminutive to gargantuan. Dozens of books have been written on the subject—philosophical treatises, picture books, and how-to books are available. Plans are obtainable from the pages of *Mother Earth News* or *Southern Living* or one of the many log home magazines that are published every month. In some ways, "log livers" have become a subculture all of their own. Packages and kits are available, and there are builders and architects who specialize in this construction type. In some places, it is still possible to cut logs on your own property and build your own cabin from them, as Virginia Huidekoper did (see page 88).

A log structure has an inherent coziness brought on by the color and texture of the timbers themselves as well as the high insulation value they possess. There is a sense of solidness and security when you are bunked down in a room built out of whole trees that have been peeled, notched, and stacked on their sides. These feelings are heightened, however, if you build a low-slung, traditional cabin with a moderately pitched roof instead of one that has high, vaulted ceilings and two-story spaces.

There are also some unique challenges presented by log construction. Wiring and plumbing are more formidable tasks if you want those utilities hidden inside the walls. Drying logs shrink considerably, so depending on their age and moisture content at the time of construction, different techniques have to be used to mitigate their movement.

Should you choose log construction for your retreat, it would be a good idea to familiarize yourself with the history and the technology of this method before beginning, and then answer this question: What specifically is the reason I personally want to build out of logs? This is a good question to ask not only about logs but for all of the following types of structures and construction.

Wood-frame Construction

Wood-platform framing (floor joists, subfloor, stud walls, ceiling joists, rafters, and roof) is an invention of the industrial age and is the most common form of residential construction in America today. Its techniques, compared to other types of wood construction, require less skill, and the various components are light enough and small enough to be handled by one or two persons. Wood studs, plywood, and framing joists are available just about anywhere, and the construction can be accomplished with hand tools (admittedly more slowly) or with power tools. The rash of do-it-yourself homebuilding stores springing up across the country are a ready source of materials, tools, and "free" advice for potential self-builders.

Though seemingly economical for the end

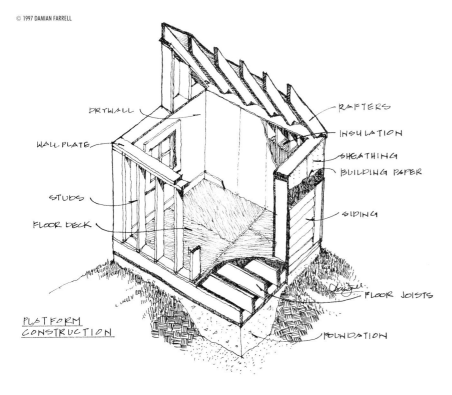

© 1997 DAMIAN FARRELL

PLATFORM
CONSTRUCTION

DRYWALL

WALL PLATE

STUDS

FLOOR DECK

RAFTERS

INSULATION

SHEATHING

BUILDING PAPER

SIDING

FLOOR JOISTS

FOUNDATION

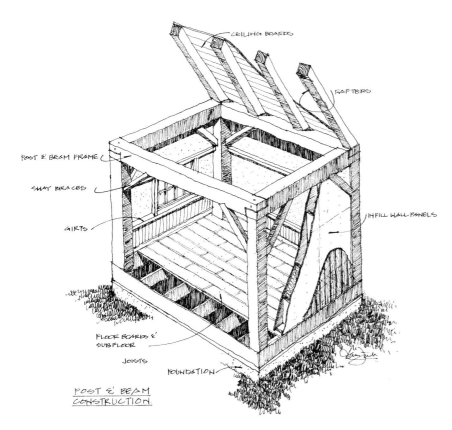

POST & BEAM
CONSTRUCTION

CEILING BOARDS

RAFTERS

POST & BEAM FRAME

SWAY BRACES

GIRTS

INFILL WALL PANELS

FLOOR BOARDS &
SUBFLOOR

JOISTS

FOUNDATION

consumer, this form of framing is relatively cost-ly from the point of view of waste, natural resources, and energy consumption. In his book *A Good House,* author Richard Manning presents a compelling description of the common 2 x 4, the amount of wood wasted in its production and making it "uniform," and the energy expended in getting raw materials and final product from here to there to here again. If one feels strongly about earth sustainability issues, this type of construction raises some interesting issues and questions.

A lesser-used method called post-and-beam or timber-frame predates platform construction. It is a series of massive vertical posts holding hefty horizontal beams that in turn support pitched-roof beams. Though it requires more care and carpentry experience, post-and-beam construction presents certain advantages over platform framing. Because the structure is supported around the perimeter, interior walls are not required for structural support; thus, more interior flexibility is gained. Posts and beams can be left exposed, providing visual interest, and can frequently be milled locally, thus providing economic opportunity and community connection for the retreat builder. A modified post-and-beam construction technique was used for Terry Baird's Montana cabin (see page 105).

Rammed-earth Construction

Compressed-earth construction techniques have a history that dates back thousands of years. There are numerous examples of earth structures around the United States—from Florida to New Mexico, from California to South Carolina—some of which have been standing for well over a hundred years.

The basic components of rammed-earth construction are a clay-and-sand soil mix, forms the width of the wall being built, and something to tamp, or "ram," the earth into its compressed state. Forms (like giant modeling clay molds) made of plywood can be relatively small and can be moved along the perimeter of a wall while it is being constructed. The soil mix can be moved with a wheelbarrow and shovel or with a backhoe or front-end loader. Tamping can be done with the south end of a digging iron, just like you would tamp in a wooden fence post (hard work!), or a small pneumatic pounder can be employed. Walls may be left as is or finished with a variety of plasters, depending on use, personal preference, and exposure to weather. The finished buildings are not dirty, and they can receive many of the same interior floor finishes (ceramic tile, carpet, vinyl tile) as one might have in a "normal" structure.

Advantages of rammed-earth construction are numerous. The actual construction material is "dirt cheap," and though some attention has to be paid to the clay and sand ratios, the material can be easily obtained in many areas. It is strong and durable and provides good insulation. Because of wall mass and thickness, structures tend to be cool in the summer and warm in the winter. They don't rot, burn, or get eaten by wood-swallowing bugs.

The disadvantages are mostly associated with others' opinion about a building made of dirt. You want me to finance what? Where is that mud structure in our building code? How do I know it will stand up?

This construction method is labor-intensive, but depending on whose labor it is could represent a significant savings over traditional frame construction. Particularly for a small retreat structure where a sense of adventure and delight should prevail, rammed earth is a viable alternative.

Stone Construction

There is something elemental and secure about stone buildings. Perhaps it is an unconscious recall of mankind's prehistoric cave-dwelling roots, or perhaps it is the mass and stability that stone represents. Stone has been employed for shelter as long as women and men

© 1997 DAMIAN FARRELL

STONE RETREAT

have been putting materials together to protect themselves from the weather. Stones have been cut and hauled and lifted to create fantastic cathedrals, such as Chartres in northern France, and mysterious monuments like the Pyramids or Stonehenge.

For the builder of a small retreat, stone construction has plenty of benefits. It is fireproof, it doesn't decay (unless you choose porous stone, which soaks up water, freezes, and cracks in the winter), it doesn't support termites, and it never needs painting. Stone blends into the landscape (assuming you don't take red sandstone to gray granite country), and buildings made with it are comparatively cooler in summer and warmer in winter than their wood-framed relatives. On many sites the material is plentiful and, depending on the style of stonework chosen, can be used as is. If your site is devoid of stone, it will be a fairly expensive prospect to procure and transport enough to build even a small retreat structure.

Stone masonry is an art, and it is becoming harder and harder to find competent folks who lay stone for a living; but stone masonry isn't so hard that it can't be tried and learned by amateurs. Many claim that a therapeutic, almost magical sense comes over them as they put together building puzzles with random bits of frozen history. A friend in Salt Lake City has for years been gathering rocks and building walls and garden paths on her steeply sloped property—just for the restorative effects it has on her body and spirit. Stones can be dry-stacked or bonded together with mortar, coursed like bricks, or laid in a random pattern. One can use small pieces or great boulders, flat stones or rounded river rocks. The variety and possibilities are endless.

Most downsides have complementary upsides. So it is with stone. Although it is heavy and hard to carry, working with it gives your body needed exercise and increased strength. Stone takes time—lots of time. One cannot build a stone building in a hurry, and if you are in a hurry, the stone has a way of slowing you down. If you need your retreat finished tomorrow, stone is probably not the way to go; but if you wish to exercise your muscles and your mind, to practice patience and find your inherent creativity, it may be a good choice.

Straw-bale Construction

As with other natural building materials, people have been using thatch, grasses, and straw as shelter-building components throughout history on at least six continents. Pioneers in North America discovered, toward the end of the nineteenth century, the ease with which they could construct durable and comfortable homes. A particular concentration of bale buildings were built on that vast, grassy sea known as the Sand Hills of Nebraska. Materials were plentiful and, human ingenuity being what it is, all kinds of building types began to appear, such as homes, barns, schools, and churches.

Bale construction uses natural by-product or

Pilgrim Holiness Church in Arthur, Nebraska, is a straw-bale structure built in the Sand Hills in 1928.

An additional benefit that goes with bale construction is the community building spirit it seems to engender. The process allows participation by folks from all walks of life, young and old, skilled and unskilled. In Wilson, Wyoming, a group of people interested in investigating low-cost housing alternatives came together to build a small shed, but while they were erecting this small bale structure, they were also strengthening a bond of common concern (see page 90).

The drawbacks to bale buildings are similar to other nontraditional forms, including questions from building officials, financing institutions, and others who only like to tread in the narrow valley of the status quo. Though there is a significant body of knowledge about bale building, it is still not very common, so you might have to reach a bit farther than the local hardware store to get answers to construction questions. The straw-bale "community" is quite fervent though, and as a group seems interested in advancing the art by a willingness to help the yet uninitiated. And finally, there are all of the jokes you might have to put up with about the Three Little Pigs and the one who built his house of straw!

ADAPTED STRUCTURES

Change, metamorphose, transmogrify, transform, mutate, transfigure, modify, adjust, convert, remake, reshape, customize, refashion, restyle, variegate, vary—all are synonyms for the word *adapt*. I invite you to look them up, especially if you have a structure in mind that you are trying to picture as it changes from a caterpillar to a butterfly. The subtle differences in their meanings may give you some new and different approaches to the potentially boring and overused notion of remodeling. *Transmogrify* has connotations of fantastic or bizarre, while *variegate* has to do with changing appearance by marking with different colors. Getting the picture yet? Different vantage points and different

waste materials, compressed, stacked, and plastered to create walls that are solid and durable, have character, and are easy to shape into many different forms. Structures can be made to look "normal" or they can take advantage of the plasticity of the natural material and be contoured into many different and delightful profiles. Bales have a high insulation value, so buildings made from them have a high degree of thermal efficiency, thus saving energy and money. Depending on the complexity of the structure, significant initial and life-cycle cost savings can be made using bales.

ideas are worth considering, especially when you are thinking about creating a special and personal retreat place. In some ways, adapting an existing structure for a different use requires an altered state of mind. It requires imagination, some risk, and an unlimited attitude about what something could be if . . .

Especially for relatively small retreat places, there are vast opportunities for creative adaptation. Almost anything that encloses space can be considered a candidate for metamorphosis. A discarded screen gazebo turned into a cabin (see page 43), an old log outbuilding refashioned into an outdoor cookhouse (see page 73), and an aging trailer house variegated into an artist studio and painted to look like logs (see page 98)—all are examples of an imaginative spirit connected with someone else's rubbish. Look around you and imagine the possibilities. What could you do with an old fallout shelter, travel trailer, or even a dumpster? What is the potential in a retired run-in shed, a chicken coop, or a discarded houseboat?

For sure, less adventuresome adaptions and renovations are perfectly acceptable for accomplishing a place for personal retreat. Putting carpet on the floor of the tack room, moving

the saddles out, and moving in an easy chair can certainly meet the definition of a haven for some. Sweeping out an old potting shed, putting on a coat of paint, and hanging an old-fashioned candelabra (with real candles, of course) will work for others. In the upstairs of her log cabin home, Virginia Huidekoper has a simple workshop where she produces fine musical instruments (see page 88). Little adaptation or decoration were required for the quality of space and experience she desired. Michael Nourot adapted a pickup-truck camper by

A sheep wagon converted into a portable bath-room/spa could be used in conjunction with a small cabin or as a stand-alone retreat.

Inside, the sheep wagon bathroom is festooned with a salvaged galvanized bathtub.

Olle Lundberg, an architect and metal sculptor, purchased a used 1962 Airstream trailer, gutted it, redesigned and transformed the interior, and hung it inside of his San Francisco studio as an office retreat.

PHOTO COURTESY OLLE LUNDBERG

mounting it to a somewhat permanent base outside of his glassmaking studio (see page 121). That's it. In over fifteen years of ownership, he has never altered the decor or the murals that were installed by the original owner.

One of the advantages of adaptive reuse is the significant cost savings that can be realized. Recently I contemplated building a small home office in which to write and from which to operate my consulting practice. I put an ad in my local newspaper for a "well-used Airstream trailer," and within a week I had two calls. I was offered a 1950s model for $1,000 and a 1960s model for $2,000. That's almost 200 square feet of interior space that could be acquired for between $5 and $10 per foot—dry, sleek, and with heating and basic electrical systems already in place. In this particular case, another $5 to $15 per foot would complete the project and I could have a high-style mobile office for under $25 per foot. In the case of my own Montana retreat (see page 42), I purchased the basic screen gazebo for $1,500—16' x 20' for $4.39 per square foot! A great deal compared to what it would cost to build from scratch.

Another meaningful benefit to converted or reshaped spaces is that of recycling whole groups of materials instead of sending them to the local landfill or the corner of your neighbor's property to slowly decompose and provide a sore sight for eyes for years to come. For instance, a used travel trailer is sheathed with aluminum siding, is on a steel frame, and is full of copper wire, copper pipes, and glass windows. All of these are materials we are encouraged to recycle from our kitchens every week. It's not so easy to put that old trailer in a blue plastic bag by the roadside for Wednesday's pick-up though! So, if adaptation doesn't appeal to you because of its practical pluses, consider it part of your social responsibility.

This salvaged screened gazebo was purchased for $1,500 then adapted to become the core of a comfortable but small retreat cabin (see p. 42).

This potential mobile office was available for only $2,000.

SALVAGED STRUCTURES OR PARTS

Whether you consider it treasure hunting or just saving discarded material for further use, and whether you are building from the ground up or adapting an existing structure for a different use, salvaged materials can come into the picture when building a retreat. Since most people are likely to be more adventuresome or playful when creating a retreat space, they are more willing to consider previously owned materials as a utilitarian or artistic addition to their hideaway.

Architectural salvage is available almost everywhere. Most cities of any size have warehouses or emporiums whose business it is to collect, sometimes refurbish, and resell salvaged materials. Building contractors, and especially demolition contractors, are a good source. Keeping a keen eye on your neighborhood, your county roads, or your city streets can result in salvage opportunities.

The kitchen in this cabin retreat owes its timeworn look to cabinets made from old pieces of furniture and a refrigerator veneered with wood siding.

Many cast-iron tubs on feet have been literally put out to pasture as stock watering tanks. This one was brought back to life and serves its original purpose. On the wall is evidence that a watchful eye and a sharp pocket-knife can provide economical wall hooks.

Humanity has a warehouse of old building materials, which they auction once or twice a year to raise money for building affordable housing. Salvage is everywhere; you just have to tune your eyes and brain to see it.

The salvaged *components* most commonly reused on construction projects include windows, doors, wood columns, plumbing fixtures, lighting fixtures, and hardware. Salvaged *materials* include roofing, woodwork, logs, structural elements, masonry units, and stone. Almost anything that is not broken, rotted, or completely rusted out can be creatively reused for something, though not always for the purpose for which it was originally intended. Stephanie Sandston used wood from her old chicken coop to build kitchen cabinets (see page 129), and Jim Raper built an outdoor bread oven from bricks bought at a local auction (see page 113). Twenty-five years ago, I helped my employer at that time to haul thousands of pounds of stone from the site of Marguerite's, a demolished "house of ill repute," to be used in turn for building exterior garden walls within the boundaries of the most exclusive neighborhood in town.

Sometimes owners are willing to sell, and sometimes they are just happy to be rid of the "trash" and will give it away to someone who is willing to haul it off. Remembering the old adage that one person's trash is another's treasure, even your local landfill can produce bounty for the discriminating hunter; but be sure to check local laws and regulations regarding wandering around a public landfill. Our local chapter of Habitat for

Salvage doesn't only apply to former buildings. Deadfall in a nearby lodgepole-pine forest can be used for porch railings, rafters, beams, columns, and furniture. If you wander onto others' property, be sure to get permission before hauling, and if on government land, you will need a permit to remove deadfall—no live trees please!

Reclamation doesn't apply only to components or materials. Whole buildings can be moved either as is, or disassembled and reassembled on a new site. When one is planning a small retreat place, this becomes a viable option because the size of the structure to be moved can be small enough to make it economically feasible. There are numerous reliable house-moving companies that specialize in jacking it up, loading it up, moving it, and putting it back down on a new foundation.

By its nature, rooting around in old buildings or piles of former buildings has its inherent dangers. Broken glass, rusty nails, rotting timbers, and hidden caches of old paint or insecticide all present opportunities for accidents to occur. All of the standard safety procedures apply and should be followed. Here are a few, but no list could cover them all: Wear goggles; wear gloves; don't lift objects that are too heavy for you; have an up-to-date tetanus shot; wear sturdy boots; make sure the electricity is *off*; remove nails from boards as you go; pay attention; and use good common sense. Demolition sites probably aren't as dangerous as driving through some cities today, but safety and attentiveness are required in order to prevent accidents from spoiling your day.

The pluses associated with reclaimed components and materials are numerous. In addition to the obvious environmental issues, recycled ingredients can add interest and value, may be (but are not always) cheaper, and can always stimulate good after-dinner stories and conversation. The drawbacks are the related unknowns, fitting challenges, and unreliable replacement

A watchful eye while searching for materials and the playful nature of retreat structures can be combined for some interesting details like this "offset" newel post.

Stacked logs, carefully numbered before being taken down, can be easily matched and restacked in a new location.

sources that are inherent in the idea of salvage. Some items, because of their rarity, popularity, or designation by dealers as "antiques," have gotten more expensive than comparable new ones. One can't always calculate the structural integrity or guarantee the exact ingredients of retrieved materials. If the Good Housekeeping Seal of Approval, U.S.D.A., or F.D.A. labels are important to you, salvage will probably make you nervous.

It took a crew of five approximately two hours to dismantle this old log cabin and load it onto two pickup trucks to be moved to its new home 45 miles away.

The restacked logs are getting a new roof and begin to take shape as a 15' x 16½' retreat studio.

PORTABLE STRUCTURES

Portable structures have their origination in necessity, not in convenience. As long as women and men have needed to move to new game-filled hunting grounds or to fresh grazing lands, they have devised ways to create shelter to carry along with them. Tents, tipis, yurts, and even covered wagons have had a role in these migrations of people and their movable homes.

Trailers and RVs

Today's easily recognized symbol for contemporary road nomads are the vacation travel trailer, the pickup-truck camper, and the self-contained recreational vehicle or RV. Thousands of these transportable retreats roam the roads across the land. They range from miniature to huge, new to used, and moderately priced to exceeding the cost of a small cottage in the south of France. For those who prefer the mystique and cowboy spirit of navigating the roads and a constantly changing retreat environment, this kind of "camping" makes perfect sense. It can be done economically and provides many the opportunity to have incredibly beautiful retreat sites that would never be possible to own.

Those who prefer this particular type of retreat structure but desire a bit more permanency (or less driving) often choose to park their trailer or RV in a stationary location. Small communities of recreational vehicle owners have sprung up across the country, where folks can purchase or "time share" a small piece of land and share services and amenities with their neighbors. And for others, a well-worn trailer parked miles from anywhere becomes a perfect permanent cabin retreat. These often have the advantage of being relatively cheap, quick to install, compact, and with most of the conveniences one could desire in such a small space. Such a core structure can be modified or supplemented with outdoor amenities or activities (hot tub, sauna, woodshed, barbecue pit), which greatly expands, from an overall-use point of view, the relatively small enclosed space.

Sheep Wagons

A variation on the trailer theme but with a more historic and romantic bent is the renovation of old sheep wagons into tiny furniture-like mobile retreats. Over the last hundred years, these wagons were found across the Great Plains and served as hearth and home to those sturdy sheepherders who cared for sizable bands of wandering wool. The original wagon was mobile, cozy, and all-inclusive, with a kitchen, woodstove, bed, and enough cupboards to store the paraphernalia needed to keep a herder going for six months at a time. Montana Wagons, a small company in McLeod, Montana, which does one-of-a-kind renovations, calls their portables "an old tradition, refined" (see page 100). Among the many uses they have explored for the wagons are a playhouse, a kitchen, a wildlife observatory, a studio, an office, a guest room, a fishing cabin, a pond cabin, a library, and a "love nest." Their literature says that their wagons can be "electrified, plumbed, telephoned, faxed, flushed, cooked, cooled, and heated." Lots of possibilities with a menu of creature comforts. That about says it all.

Wall Tents

"I have this affection for wall tents because they are so wound in the history of the settlement of the West," says Bob Jonas, who owns several backcountry wall-tent retreats in the mountains north of Ketchum, Idaho (see page 136). He recalls mining camps, early cow towns, and hunting camps. Others have memories of Boy Scout camp, family vacations, a first deer hunt, or even military service experiences. Wall tents evoke memories and often pleasant associations with the past, and they provide easy, affordable opportunities for someone to own a personal retreat space without spending a life savings in the process.

Lightweight, mobile, and inexpensive, wall tents can provide retreat shelter at a fraction of the cost of more permanent structures of the same size. A 16' x 20' tent with a center ridge-pole height of 9' 9", made of 12-ounce water-proofed and flame-retardant canvas, can be purchased for under $1,000, or around $3 per square foot. In tents, canvas is a preferred material because it has more resistance to the damaging ultraviolet rays of the sun and will last many times longer than nylon. A woodstove can be installed for heat, and cots or bunks can provide comfortable sleeping arrangements.

For more permanence and stability, a wall tent can be placed over a wooden frame built on top of a wooden platform, which in effect becomes a canvas-covered cabin. These structures can be built as stationary platforms or can be designed so that they can be towed from location to location when the owner desires a change of scenery.

The Breteche Creek Guest Ranch, just west of Cody, Wyoming, has taken wall tents to the next step. Their guest accommodations are what they describe as "wooden cabins with canvas roofs." They are complete with screened doors and rugs on the floor and sleep from one to four persons. The ranch chooses to operate these "cabins" without electricity in order to emphasize the stunning natural environment that envelops the area. It's not the usual image one thinks of when the term *dude ranch* comes up, but their bookings indicate that many folks like, and even prefer, these kinds of accommodations.

Best-selling author Annie Dillard extols the virtues of retreating simply. For her, that means an 8' x 10' prefabricated toolshed at her winter residence and a 9' x 12' canvas wall tent at her summer home. Her wall-tent luxury is a sewn-in floor to keep out the varmints, but after that it is furnished simply with a desk, a cot, and an extension cord to provide power for her word processor. She sees her retreat as a healthy escape from the confines of her house, and

A wall tent dining room with an outdoor kitchen.

A modified wall tent with wooden sides and a screened door is built on a moveable platform that can be relocated at will.

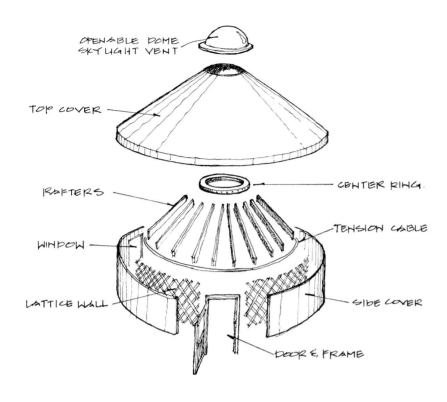

OPENABLE DOME
SKYLIGHT VENT

TOP COVER

RAFTERS

CENTER RING

WINDOW

TENSION CABLE

LATTICE WALL

SIDE COVER

DOOR & FRAME

© 1997 DAMIAN FARRELL

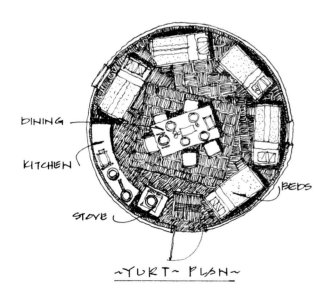

DINING

KITCHEN

BEDS

STOVE

~YURT~ PLAN~

though she works there every day, the fanciful nature of the place keeps her fresh and alive. "When you build a fancy study—a houselet—or add a room to your house, you lose the fun of the thing. A toolshed or a tent, like a tree house, lets you fool yourself into thinking you are not working, only playing." (Annie Dillard, "Keeping It Simple," *Architectural Digest,* June 1996, p. 36.)

Yurts

"Yurt power" is how Bob Jonas describes it (see page 139). "People are looking for something that has an inspirational quality to it, and yurts have that," says Allen Bair, owner of Pacific Yurts, a commercial producer in Cottage Grove, Oregon. With their round form, light lattice walls, slender wood rafters, translucent skin, and skylight at the conical apex, yurts do exude enchanting qualities of creativity, adventure, and romance. Entering a yurt makes one feel somehow different—and special.

The Mongolian yurt has been around since the time of Genghis Khan, and its heritage is associated with the nomads of the high Asian plateaus. Though the technology has changed somewhat, the form and structural design of the yurt has remained essentially the same. Goat skins have been replaced with high-tech, fireproof, UV-resistant vinyl coverings, but the basic concept has endured—that of a comfortable, lightweight, mobile structure that can be erected in a relatively short time by just a couple of people. Most are pitched on permanent wooden platforms, but when circumstances insist, they can be taken down, loaded up, and moved in the back of a pickup or on a sled pulled by a snowmobile to be placed in a new location.

Yurts can be insulated so that a high level of comfort exists in both temperature extremes. Woodstoves make them toasty in winter, and their natural ventilation system keeps them cool in the summer. Interior finishes can range from the rough planks of the base platform to hardwood floors covered with ancient oriental rugs and everything in between. Some choose yurts for retreats, studios, or ski huts, and others turn them into guest houses or full-time residences.

Available in diameters from 12' to 30', yurts can provide a space the size of a small bedroom up to the area of a small house. They are produced commercially by a number of companies and can also be built from scratch. A 30'-diameter yurt can be purchased for around $7,500. After adding shipping costs, an insulation package, a good-quality woodstove, and a wooden-base platform, the total costs will still be well under $25 per square foot—just a fraction of the cost of conventional construction.

Bair, who started his company by building a yurt for his personal use, says, "Everybody has in mind a special place where they'd like to go or where they'd like to do something, but because of the cost involved, many people never do it. A yurt allows those dreams to manifest themselves."

• • •

Allen Bair sums up the experience of many as he remembers the cherished retreat place of his youth. "I grew up going to Lake Superior country. My grandparents had a little cabin there, and I remember my grandmother washing me in the sink. I remember my grandfather making a fire and listening to the shortwave radio. When I go to relax in my mind, I go to that which was their family retreat. Everybody has a special place in their mind."

Bair and others mentioned in these pages haven't tried to duplicate those places or those experiences, but they have pursued an inner calling to make a place of their own.

The aforementioned construction types and examples only scratch the surface of the world of possibilities. I hope you can use them as idea generators to jump-start your brain into action as you begin to dream, to plan, and to realize your own personal retreat.

Light plays across the spacious interior of a yurt being used as summer staff quarters at the Breteche Creek Guest Ranch.

LAST CONTACT

"Shall I go to heaven or go a-fishing?"

THOREAU

Rewards of the river.

PHOTO © 1997 LAWSON DRINKARD

THE FONDEST MEMORIES I have of outdoor adventures with my father are of hunting and fishing, which he dearly loved and shared with me. I loved my dad, I love fishing, and fishing is what drew me to Montana and eventually to the base of Contact Mountain, a 9,000-foot peak in the Gallatin National Forest.

In the early 1980s, my wife Suzanne and I were rabid college basketball fans, and the team we were following at the time was ranked number one in the country and were odds-on favorites to win the coveted NCAA Championship. Fate had a different plan, however, for the team and for us. A loss in the NCAA tournament took our team out of the running for the title and caused us to cancel a trip we had planned to the Final Four in Albuquerque. We decided instead to satisfy a long-held yearning to travel to Montana. The spring creeks and big rivers of Montana are a siren's song for those who love the pursuit of the wily trout.

I claim a genetic connection to the West. My great-grandfather, Frank Buch, and his wife Julia were homesteaders in Powell, Wyoming, in the early part of this century. When I was young, many of the stories I learned in my grandmother's lap centered around her youthful experiences in the wild Wyoming country. Ice skating on the irrigation canals, my great-grandfather building the Presbyterian church in Powell, tornadoes across the prairie, and a vacation trip around Yellowstone National Park in a covered wagon were all part of the lore. I have always cherished my familial connection to the West and believe I was unconsciously looking for a way to resolve the geographical tension.

So it was a passion for fly-fishing and a pio-neer heritage, along with a healthy dose of providence, that led us to our retreat now known as the Last Contact Ranch.

In the early years, our visits to Montana were for one week, then ten days, two weeks, then three and a little longer to drink in enough of the mountains and streams, horses and wild-flowers, and the independent spirit and neigh-borly way of life to keep us going for the other eleven months of the year. We yearned to scatter some of our own seed and put down some roots that would bind us to this country in a way that several weeks on a guest ranch just couldn't sat-isfy. We felt a need to make a commitment to the land, our neighbors, and to ourselves. Besides, it had been a long-term personal goal to

This cozy cabin is an adapted screen gazebo. Plywood siding was replaced with locally milled fir board and batten siding, and screens were replaced with inexpensive barn-sash windows. A split-face concrete-block foundation was used to give the appearance of stone.

This gable end of the cabin faces the river and mountain beyond, which rises 3,000 feet above the surface of the water. "Saddlebag" spaces attached to both sides of the original building make room for a kitchen and bath on the back and a sittin' porch on the front.

own land adjacent to a trout stream, and that aspiration was calling me forward.

After several years of searching, we were again blessed by good fortune when a tract of land became available, located immediately adjacent to a ranch owned and operated by our dearest Montana friends, Jeane and Steve Aller. Though it was a complicated transaction—and not without risk and worry—we decided to purchase this acreage, which met most of our criteria for a perfect retreat place. It has river frontage on superb trout water; it is secluded and hidden yet accessible from a "main" gravel road; it is thirty-one miles from town; and one could spend a lifetime appreciating the subtle physical beauty of the surrounding landscape. For us, it is our earthly Eden.

A band of barn-sash windows bring in the maximum outside light and take best advantage of the magnificent views beyond. The bottom chord of the existing 2' x 6' framing trusses are left exposed.

Common-grade unfinished pine covers the interior wall and ceiling surfaces, making a convenient backdrop for a continuously changing collection of western art. The existing pine floor has been sanded and oiled. Lighting for the dining area/quilting studio/office /art gallery is provided by a simple metal light fixture plugged into a duplex electrical outlet wired to a wall switch.

The compact kitchen includes a 24"-wide electric stove and oven, a stacked washer and dryer, a 30"-wide refrigerator, and a single-bowl sink. Ceiling lights are simple porcelain fixtures with 4"- round "fancy" light bulbs purchased at the local hardware store.

This 8' x 16' woodshed was built of fir boards at a local sawmill and brought to the site in one piece on a flatbed truck. It is an economical solution to wood, mower, and tool storage—or it could become the shell for a small retreat.

An exterior closet houses a 55-gallon hot-water heater, the "key" for turning on and off the valve in the 4'-deep water line, and hoses and antifreeze for winterizing the cabin. In addition to saving precious interior space, its exterior location makes the water heater easier to drain and not so messy should it ever develop a leak.

Barn-sash windows come in a variety of stock sizes. Wooden stops are built into the window frame and are held in place with wooden blocks cut on an angled kerf. Window screens are built into the frame and remain permanently in place. These windows can be lifted completely out for cleaning or for more ventilation.

So we had a splendid piece of property but no cabin, no cottage, no abode—and no funds to jump right in and build something new. We considered various alternatives, including a wall tent, a used travel trailer, and other temporary structures. Small and cheap were our primary criteria.

While scouting the real estate prior to purchase, I had noticed an old freestanding screen gazebo sitting off in a secluded grove of trees and in the beginning stages of disintegration. It was 16' x 20' with a split-cedar shake roof, textured plywood siding, and an unfinished pine floor. The perimeter was banded with insect screen—a genuine indoor-outdoor space. Over the course of its career, the gazebo had lived in several places. Its most famous visitor had apparently been former New York Yankees manager Billy Martin, and according to local legend, "Billy Martin once slept here." If it could be moved before, it could be moved again, and as a practicing architect with a healthy ego, I said to myself—and within earshot of witnesses— "I can make a cabin out of this." A deal was struck, and for $1,500 Suzanne and I owned lots of promise and the skeleton of our future cabin.

In my architectural practice I had been accustomed to drawing and documenting projects in great detail. It was not unusual to produce eight to ten 24" x 36" sheets of drawings for even the smallest house or addition. These would be accompanied by a 50- to 100-page book of specifications detailing everything from plumbing fixtures to door hinges to termite protection and roof flashing. Distance, time, custom, humor, and attitude dictated that I approach this project differently. I would be 2,000 miles from the cabin while much of the construction was occurring. I didn't have the time to make ten sheets of drawings for a personal project. That's not the way things get built in this valley anyway, and I wasn't in the humor to pursue it "normally." I was interested in a different, less stressful method for this building process. If it was going to be a retreat, it needed to be approached not like a job but rather like an endeavor that would be an energy maker, not an energy taker.

First there were the issues of time, schedule, and money. We didn't have a cabin and we wanted one as soon as possible. But we lived many miles away and didn't have the required cash to do a turnkey project. We had to resist the temptation to apply the get-it-done, instant-gratification attitudes so common today at work and at home and take a more leisurely, deliberate approach. Sometimes—in fact, often—good things take time to work themselves out. After all, it took Michelangelo eight years to paint the ceiling of the Sistine chapel. By necessity, we decided on a pay-as-you-go plan. Save some money, dig a footing and lay a foundation; save a little more and take the next step. We were fortunate to become acquainted with Gene and Catherine Stuber, a local couple who worked together on small construction projects in our valley and were willing to fit our erratic schedule into theirs. They built our entire cabin using one simple floor plan drawing that was produced on an 8½" x 11" piece of paper. The rest of the communications were oral. A handshake, trust, communication, and the right spirit got this retreat built, not contracts, lawyers, and detailed documentation.

The original gazebo building was 400 square feet, which we felt was almost, but not quite, enough space for the three members of the Drinkard family. After many rough sketches and a few family meetings, we finally arrived at an acceptable and quite concise floor plan. Three "saddlebags" would be added to the basic rectangle. On one of the long sides, an 8' x 12' space was added to accommodate the kitchen and bathroom. One gable end accepted the addition of a 10' x 12' bedroom, and to the other long side was added a roofed porch. Our one-bedroom cabin with a quite compact kitchen and bathroom totals only 536 square feet. The

original main space accommodates a woodstove that heats the whole place, a dining table that doubles as my desk and Suzanne's quilting studio, and a fold-down futon couch that becomes our daughter's bedroom at night.

Once we decided on the basic plan, we were ready to begin. My friend and neighbor Steve brought his tractor with the portable backhoe, and together we dug the foundation footings and trenches for electric and water lines—really he dug and I pointed a lot. The frost line is deep in Montana, so these were actually 4'-deep ditches. Soon after the "dig," Gene and Catherine laid a split-face block (which looks like stone) foundation, loaded our gazebo onto a flatbed trailer, hooked it to their truck, and moved it to its new home.

Economy and simplicity were the order of the day as we proceeded with the construction. Fir boards were milled at the local sawmill for the exterior siding; a used hot-water heater was obtained from a neighbor; the existing pine floor was sanded and oiled but not finely finished. The bottoms of the 2' x 6' roof trusses in the gazebo were left exposed; common grade unfinished pine was used for interior wall and ceiling surfaces; a tin roof was used for the additions; and simple barn-sash windows were used throughout. The front door was built on-site and, rather than a store-bought doorknob set, has a sliding, flat steel bar that acts as the latch. The interior doors, also built there, have simple surface-mounted colonial-style latches. The bathroom shower was "previously owned," and the plumbing system was designed to drain completely by opening just one valve in the shallow crawl space. It takes about half an hour to completely winterize and put the cabin to bed for the long, cold season.

We were extravagant in only two places, and they both had to do with staying warm. First, we decided to insulate the floor, walls, and ceiling, even though it was our original intention only to use the cabin in the summer. That plan

Lawson, Suzanne, and Sarah Drinkard.

has since changed, and when the snow flies, we are glad to have that extra thermal assistance. Second, we invested in a top-quality wood-stove. Suzanne wanted to be able to see the burning fire, so this stove is designed with glass doors in the front. It has a catalytic converter, is air-tight and highly efficient. Properly stoked at bedtime, it will keep us warm all night long with no 3:00 A.M. trips to the woodpile being necessary.

Our cabin will never be finished, that's part of the plan. But after it was finally inhabitable, we began the joyous project of making it reflect who and what we are, and placed in and around it the visual anchors that help create the state of mind called retreat. For Suzanne, those include hanging flower baskets and a cottonwood log hollowed out for summer geraniums, a river-rock walk leading from the driveway to our porch, a hummingbird feeder, and a small herb garden. She has also taught herself to build lodgepole-pine furniture, which has taken forms such as a telephone stand, benches, side tables, and picture frames for treasured art. Together we built the bookshelves using aged 3"-thick planks from a nearby ranch sawmill and pine poles from a friend's furniture-building stash. For me those anchors include such simple things as our fly rods hanging on two nails over the porch in a constant state of readiness for a rising trout, a lodgepole-pine bed made by a friend down the road, my Great-great-grandfather Buch's cobbler tools hanging on the wall, and an outdoor wood-fired hot tub for cool evenings and howling at the moon.

Though the cabin is small, it is not limiting. In fact, its size makes it unbridling in many ways. Careful choices have to be made about what to bring in, what to purchase, what to keep, and what to reject. Simple pleasures abound, and they are not cluttered or dictated by "stuff." Morning coffee, a walk up the road, or an occasional visit by a big bull moose enrich our lives and add meaning. No television brings a daily diet of bad news or disgusting talk shows with invented perversions. The newspaper only comes when we decide to purchase it, and the mail is delivered just three times a week.

A favorite quote, credited in my collection to Alfred A. Montepert, says, "The environment you fashion out of your thoughts, your beliefs, your ideals, your philosophy, is the only climate you will ever live in." The Last Contact is a place to reflect on those things, so that the way we live our lives is right-spirited and constantly questioned. And then there is the fishing that first lured us there. The river, no matter how familiar it has become, always beckons with the promise of that yet unchallenged trout.

A circular wood hot tub made of western red cedar is heated with a submersible aluminum woodstove. Kits for these tubs—easy to use and to maintain (no moving parts to break down)—are available in various sizes. The seats in this tub face Contact Mountain, which is a relaxing backdrop while having a late-night soak.

CANYON TREE HOUSE

The drop of rain maketh a hole in the stone, not by violence, but by oft falling.

HUGH LATIMER

MICHAEL RYPIEN has rich childhood memories, a vivid dream, little extra cash, and indefatigable persistence. And he has a tree house on the side of a busy canyon road.

While growing up with a father who was in the military service, Rypien, his brother, and his dad built a small retreat cabin in the Uintas, a mountain range in northeastern Utah. Though the cabin is no longer in the family, Rypien still owns the spirit of the place and his experiences there. He is on a quest to build his own retreat place so that his children might have the opportunity to someday cherish memories and experiences similar to his own.

As a divorced father of three boys, Rypien is slowly working away at his dream of creating a place for recreation and retreat with his sons. As a dreamer he knows what he wants. As a realist he knows what he can afford. He has decided not to let his current reality get in the way of his powerful dream.

Perched high on a hillside overlooking the highway and river beyond, Michael Rypien's small tree house is constructed from a variety of leftover materials from friends' construction sites.

Railroad ties act as a retaining wall, enabling the hillside to be pushed back to make more flat space for family activities. The single window is set in a handmade wooden frame.

The deck and secure railing are built with new store-bought wood. Folding lawn chairs and a milk crate are the only deck furniture.

For two years, Rypien combed legal notices and scoured tax records looking for an affordable way to purchase a piece of property on the trout-filled Ogden River, which tumbles and slides down the beautiful Ogden Canyon. With a multitude of opportunities for hiking, biking, skiing, boating, and fishing, this area is one of the major outdoor recreational playgrounds for those in the Salt Lake City/Ogden vicinity. His diligence and patience finally paid off, and he was able to purchase three contiguous lots—one at a public tax auction and the other two from Weber County for the payment of back taxes. His land holdings now total a whopping one-half acre—a combined lot that is only 103 feet by 210 feet. But he has only $8,000 invested and points out that quarter-acre lots in town frequently sell for more than five times as much.

Before Rypien's purchase, the land was not the kind of site that beckoned to most as a spot for a potential family retreat. The property is narrow, steep, and sits below a large, exposed water pipeline that serves the next valley to the north. At the time of purchase, it was heavily wooded and had no appreciable flat space on it. But Rypien could see qualities that others drove past. "One of the main reasons I purchased it was because my father and I used to fish the river and enjoy this canyon." After many months of hard physical labor with a chain saw and a rented backhoe, he created a clear flat site next to the road and began planning for a small cabin and a place to picnic and to play volleyball and basketball with his kids.

Almost four years later, the retreat has the beginnings of a 4'-high rock wall to create separation from the highway, a basketball backboard without a net or rim, and a small tree house and deck hanging about twenty-five feet above the ground.

At one time the retreat had a basketball court, a picnic area, and a shed for equipment,

A metal-clad door is not usually associated with a rustic mountain retreat but fits nicely into Rypien's palette of materials. Care and sure feet are required to navigate the steep path and stairs.

alternative plan—a tree house. After calling city hall and finding no ordinance preventing the construction of such, he disassembled the shed and transformed it into a tree house, cleverly wedged between the limbs of a tree and the steep hillside that rises behind it. "It is less than 10' x 10', so you don't need a building permit for it. The city has no recourse because there is nothing on the books that says you cannot have a tree house." As the city officials consider the tree house, he says, "They really don't know what to do with me."

When he refers to those at city hall with whom he disagrees, it is only in kind terms and polite language, with never a cross word. But Rypien believes that the city does not want him to build there. There are disagreements about setbacks and septic percolation rates. Now it seems that another regulation requiring a minimum size of a one-acre lot for residential buildings in the canyon is trying to get in the way. Rypien believes he has a legal right to build a cabin on his property because of certain grandfather clauses in the zoning ordinance. He is not interested in a fight with the city, but at the same time he wants to build his cabin on his land. The tree house is a temporary retreat until that goal can be accomplished.

So what started out to be a cabin retreat with a basketball court is now a tiny tree house with a small deck overlooking the Ogden River and the majestic mountains that rise abruptly behind it. It was built with simple hand tools and a chain saw. Though electricity is available, Rypien hasn't chosen to afford the connection fees. So far, he has used less than $100 worth of store-bought materials, preferring to make do with reclaimed materials and gifts of surplus from builder friends. The single window is set in a handmade frame and most of the finishes are rough.

For now, the tree house provides a sunny deck to visit with friends and a cozy shelter for overnight jaunts with his boys. "I have to smile, because I'm not in to it so much that I am ever

but Rypien has run into some obstacles. He says the city zoning ordinance states that one must have at least a one-acre site in order to have a "recreation area," and that without an existing residential building, one cannot have a shed. So, in order to avoid fines and possible legal actions, he took down the basketball rim and took the picnic table back to town so as not to have a recreation area. Undaunted, he came up with an

Optimism and hope for the future are evident in the installation of a circular driveway and front steps to a cabin that remains as yet unbuilt. One of Rypien's ways of enjoying his retreat is to make the land attractive for his guests and for those who are just passing by. Thus, the circular flowerbed.

going to lose anything. I'm not a cheap person, but I am thrifty."

Rypien has approached the development of his land, in some ways, like Thomas Jefferson approached the building of his beloved Monticello. He builds things and if he is not satisfied with the way they look, he takes them down and builds them again. In order to have the kind of place he wants, he is willing to be innovative and to change, and he is not in a hurry. It took Jefferson some forty years to complete Monticello. He is reported to have once said to a friend, "Architecture is my delight, and putting up and pulling down, one of my favorite amusements." The "architecture" of the tree house has no similarities to the classic designs of Mr. Jefferson, but the attitude and care about the land and the building process has some parallels. The making of the place was, and is, as important as the final product.

An old Haitian proverb says, "The oxen are slow, but the earth is patient." Sometimes the things that are most worth doing in life happen at a speed that is not by man's own design.

Because of the circumstances of his life, including the loss of a long-held job at a local mill, Mike Rypien could have a sour attitude. Instead, he is pursuing his education for a new career as a physical education teacher, being a great father to his boys, and at the same time slowly working to build his dream retreat in Ogden Canyon. When asked what advice he would offer to others who might want to build their own retreat he said, "Have patience. It should be the successes you focus on, so plug away. Don't dwell on your mistakes. Just make 'em and get on with it."

Retreat for Michael Rypien is about memories of the past and dreams for the future. His is about a place to act out both of these in the present moment and thus nourish his soul. Rypien is in this venture for the long haul. "It's just the western spirit about having a spot with a little cabin to get away with my boys. Eventually you'll see a nice little cabin here, but if all else fails, I'll dig a cave."

AN ARCHITECT'S RETREAT

*This is the true nature of home—
it is the place of Peace.*

JOHN RUSKIN

Roosting on the hillside, Vickery's cabin is anchored by an enormous rock protruding from the landscape.

ROBERT VICKERY has spent his entire career considering the important issues of how we put buildings upon the land. As a teacher in the concepts of architecture and design, he shared his philosophy with, and learned from, thousands of students. As an author, he has written on the philosophy of architecture and on planning the human landscape. As a practitioner, he has designed hundreds of buildings and dozens of different building types. But until he designed The Retreat, he had never built a new structure for himself.

In fact, the daily pressures of running a successful architectural practice and teaching a full course load at the University of Virginia School of Architecture while trying to complete his second book were part of the reason he was moved to build himself a small mountain hideaway in the Blue Ridge Mountains north of Charlottesville, Virginia.

It is not surprising that he kept several strong conceptual ideas in mind when designing and building his mountain retreat.

Even in the spring before the leaves are fully out, The Retreat accomplishes one of Vickery's design goals by being almost invisible from only a few paces away.

Says Vickery, "My philosophy of retreat is that it's small and it's hidden. Retreat to me does not imply a four-bedroom house with running water. That's a vacation house, and that's different. My idea philosophically of the retreat is a place one goes to get away from it all; where you are protected from the elements in the most modest way possible."

First, he wanted to make a place that was hidden and was, in fact, a retreat. He wanted it to be very small, with no utilities—no electricity, no telephone, and no plumbing. His cabin is only 12' x 12' of enclosed space attached to a similar-sized deck. Lighting is by candle and flashlight; fresh water is hauled from a nearby stream; heating is by a small woodstove; and the septic system is a pit dug nearby with a toilet seat over it—a modest accommodation with no outhouse covering it.

His second organizing idea was about a concern and respect for the land. Using his own well-defined geographic criteria, Vickery searched for his retreat property for eight years. "I always had this idea that it would be fun to have a place really in the mountains where you could commune with nature," said Vickery. He finally settled on mountainous acreage surrounded on three sides by the Shenandoah National Park, which virtually guarantees that no development will ever occur along his property borders.

After that quest was complete, it took him six more months of study and contemplation to select the cabin location. Several dramatic sites were available to him, and one in particular would have had the cabin deck hanging high over a steep drop to the stream below. "In selecting the cabin site, I did not want to despoil the wilderness. I decided not to put it there because it made too strong a statement and spoiled the edge of the bluff line from below. I wanted it to be hidden in the woods—a place you wouldn't see until you were right on it." Ultimately Vickery selected a site next to a huge protruding

Nature's throne—a truly "outdoor" toilet!

Vickery, seated in his open air "living room," muses about his philosophy of architecture as it relates to putting a cabin on the landscape.

The Retreat is open for use. A barn-style door slides open and shut on a red steel track.

rock. The cabin is nestled behind this monolith and its deck wraps around it, embracing it as a part of the structure, making a strong man-to-land connection. He says, "The cabin and the deck are like a ship anchored to this rock. You can come out in the fall, and when the mist comes down you can hardly see anything. You can wander out at night and the rock is there, holding you to this sacred place on the land. I can't think of anyplace on the acreage where I would rather have the cabin."

After eight and a half years of preparation, the actual construction of the cabin took only three weeks. A former student and apprentice architect in Vickery's firm pitched a wall tent and took up residence on the site until the building was complete. With no vehicular access, all of the construction materials and tools had to be hand carried, the last stretch up a very steep hill.

"It's very important to me that you have to leave the car behind and hike in that last quarter mile. Everything you bring in you have to hand carry. Everything you take out you have to hand carry. It makes you very carefully select what you bring in and out, and not bring too much."

The building itself accomplished the third of Vickery's conceptual notions. "Once I decided to build a cabin, I said I'd like to build one that was very clearly done by an architect." The 12'-square box is rigorously proportioned inside and out using a 5:7:12 ratio. The front wall is 12' high, sloping to 7' in the rear, giving the roof a 5 in 12 pitch. The sliding glass door is 5' x 7'.

Inside looking out from the 12' x 12' cabin space. The built-in writing desk doubles as a kitchen counter, and the loft over the sliding glass door provides additional sleeping space.

The outdoor fire ring, in good weather, serves as kitchen, dining room, and living room.

Inside, a wooden hanging strip is set at 7' high. The modular furniture, which can be arranged into a single or double bed, also adheres to the 5' x 7' proportions. Though these dimensions were carefully planned and executed, they don't scream out and call attention to themselves. It just looks right and feels good to enter this well-proportioned building.

Vickery's favorite detail is the sliding barn-style door that runs on a steel track and covers the sliding glass door when the cabin is not occupied. "The hanging wood door slides open and changes the way the whole cabin looks. When it is open, the cabin seems roomy and full of life. When you close it up, the cabin is part of the forest again." He is also fond of the 5:7:12 ratio because of the very modest reference it makes to the design of one of his architectural heroes, Frank Lloyd Wright. "It reminds me that I am an architect, and the cabin was designed by an architect."

Vickery visits The Retreat around twenty times each year. His activities revolve around hiking, cooking, and conversation. "I have seven or eight favorite hikes. They spread over a year and then I start over." Access to the Appalachian Trail is a three-mile trek, mostly uphill.

Though the cabin allows for cooking inside on the Waterford woodstove, Vickery prefers to use his outdoor fire ring, which in good weather serves as kitchen, dining room, and living room. "I wanted a place I could come out and stay one night, have a wonderful day hiking, feel good, come back to the cabin, enjoy cooking a meal, sleep overnight, get up, wash dishes, and go home. There is a kind of marvelous thing that happens to someone when you bring them up here. They seem to get a cleaner sense of life, a sense that everything is washed away. You can just sit here by this fire and talk for hours on end and it never seems to get boring. My favorite activity is to sit in that ambience and have a nice conversation and a pleasant meal with perfect assurance that nothing is going to interrupt you from beginning to end. A four-hour refresher—that's the best."

With a masterful knowledge of architectural history, Vickery frequently refers in conversation to great architects or buildings of the past. He gives a short historical overview of retreats, mentioning lavish fortresses from Chinese literature and the Villa Rotunda by Andrea Pallido—a retreat built in Vicenza, Italy, for two brothers from Venice.

But it was his personal history that, in some ways, called him to build his own hideaway and affected its design. "As a small child my parents didn't have a great deal of money. We always took our family vacations for two weeks in the Missouri Ozarks and stayed in a cabin owned by my great-aunt. The cabin slept twelve, and people would come and go. It was always such fun as a child to go floating and fishing on the river. This is very deep in my memory. I always wanted to have a cabin in the mountains. When it became time to build it, I realized I really didn't want to live in the mountains, I just wanted to come and experience them."

Vickery's advice for prospective retreat builders is consistent with the concepts he used in his own design process. "Spend the necessary time to find the right land. Think small. Think what is the smallest possible thing you can construct that will make you happy for what you want to do there. Plan your site very carefully."

Robert Vickery is a person of the mind—of education and literature and the arts. He has lived and worked in a world of ideas and philosophy and dialogue. But he has found his respite in the simpler offerings of nature—the changing seasons, the rustling trees, and the star-speckled dark of the wilderness night. "I need to have this contrast for my wholeness of life. I always feel reinvigorated when I come here. I always feel happy about nature. Nature has a peacefulness to it that is understandable. No matter what is happening in the city, nature is going its own way."

The deck, built to embrace the large "anchor" rock, has become a natural extension of the stone and has taken on a similar natural patina over time.

SOD-ROOFED SANCTUARY

The reward of a thing well done, is to have done it.

RALPH WALDO EMERSON

The uphill side of the river house is a run-in shed for the Johnsons' horses. The shed starts at the top of the hill and slopes down toward the river, allowing a retreat space on a lower level. Log slab siding gives it an "always been there" appearance.

"I CAN MOVE 500-pound things with a lever and a wedge," says Donna Johnson. "It gets me into a lot of trouble because I'm convinced that there is nothing I can't do if I just think about it. For my fiftieth birthday my two daughters wanted to give me a portable phone, but I said I wanted a circular saw instead."

Johnson's first career was a full-time homemaker and mother, nurturing and raising four children in such diverse places as California, New Mexico, Colorado, and Nebraska. Her husband Wally is an international attorney who has always traveled extensively and has had to be away from home a good deal of the time. After their children were grown and had left home to pursue their own lives, Donna and Wally decided, "We have to do something. We have to create something. We need a project—a together project."

Early retirement wasn't what they were looking for. "So many people retire, they move, they get sick, and they die," says Donna. "We wanted to get into a new life before we retired." So they

The sod roof has been carefully planted with vegetation that can survive dry summers and cold Wyoming winters.

Railroad-tie retaining walls allow the river house to be sunken into the ground, keeping it low with a very human scale. The red wagon seat is one of the many imaginative ways Johnson has used "found" objects for new purposes.

began a search for a place to launch this new phase of their lives. They had always liked the front range of the Rockies—the tall mountains and the clear rivers—but Colorado seemed a bit too crowded. Though neither can remember how they first got to Cody, Wyoming, Donna now describes it as the perfect choice. She confides, "I could be happy as a clam out here not seeing a soul for two weeks, but Wally needs to go to town. Living thirty miles outside of town satisfies her need to be out on the land, and the Whitney Museum of Western Art and Buffalo Bill Historic Center, along with the airport, provide the necessary cultural and business opportunities for Wally.

After deciding on Cody, it took the Johnsons five years to find the kind of project that suited them. Realtors, unable to find what the couple needed or unwilling to understand their dream, kept trying to show large, new, beautiful houses with spectacular landscaped yards. Donna explained to them, "I don't want a gorgeous house. I have one of those back in Omaha. I

want something I can play with and have fun with and make mine. We want somewhere we can live and gradually do projects."

They finally purchased a modest ranch house on twenty acres along the South Fork of the Shoshone River. Donna describes the house as undistinguished. "From the road we don't look like much of anything, which is fine. I like it that way." After buying the property she set about the long task of making this ordinary ranch house into the Johnson family retreat, aptly named the Lazy DW Ranch, which is actually a series of retreats including the main house, the cookhouse, the river house, a barn/bunkhouse, and a tipi that houses overflow guests, kids, and three grandkids.

Because of personal interest, aptitude, and necessity, Donna has always taken the lead on her family's home-improvement projects. In addition to mothering her children, she has made her financial contribution to the marriage by buying, rehabilitating, and reselling a series of older houses. "I did the painting, the wall-papering, the electrical and the plumbing, and we'd sell them and notch up. If you had to hire that labor, you wouldn't do as well."

At the ranch, Donna took charge of not just the planning but the hands-on doing of the renovation, construction, and land-improvement projects. After a gradual renovation of the existing main house and a library addition to house Wally's prized book collection, she took to

Taking advantage of the natural slope of the land, Johnson's retreat space is on the lower level of this run-in shed. The building accomplishes her goal of a "low, snuggly," and rustic appearance.

69

Occupying only 20 acres, the Lazy DW Ranch is modest by Wyoming ranch standards, but the view enjoyed from the banks of the Shoshone River makes the place seem much larger indeed.

Her hand bandaged from an injury sustained stacking logs in the cookhouse, Donna Johnson enthusiastically explains what her next project will be.

Johnson's genealogy wall in the river house documents family roots, home places, and history.

reclaiming the land and creating the various other retreat places on the property.

For some people the process of building is just a necessary step in order to create a place of retreat. Donna derives nourishment for her soul from the making of the places. "I can't imagine getting up in the morning without a huge list of projects," she says. Though her friend Carl Davis, a local builder, does some of the heavy construction, Donna does much of the work herself. "I'm in heaven. . . . My nails are broken, my hands are beat up, and my arthritis has set in because I overdo it. I'm just in my glory."

Though most of her building experiences have been happy ones, occasionally she has a learning episode she hadn't bargained for. Several years ago while doing some caulking,

she was stranded on a roof for several hours after her ladder blew down. She was finally rescued by a passerby and learned in the future to drive a nail and wire the ladder to the eaves while working on the roof. More recently, while putting some large logs back up on her outdoor cookhouse project, she got her hand stuck between two heavy logs. About that experience she said, as her eyes twinkled, "I've learned so much—a lot of it the hard way. I do get myself into some difficulties. I should have thought a little bit more about putting those logs up before I did it." She attributes her building knowledge and her love for tools to her father-in-law, who was an engineer. "I learned so much from him. Had he been my father, wow, who knows what I might have turned into!"

The genesis of the river house retreat came

from a practical need. After buying a couple of horses, a run-in shed was needed to protect them from the gnashing winds of the Wyoming winters. Selecting a site that sloped naturally toward the river, Donna realized that she could incorporate a cozy room on a lower level if she started the roof of the shed at the top of the hill and sloped it toward the river. Though she couldn't convince Carl to "build it crooked," she did successfully convey her idea of a "low, snuggly, old-looking building with a sod roof." After the base structure was complete and the log slabs were attached, Donna took over, finishing the inside, "planting" the roof, and designing a stone mural for the inside of the screened porch. The interior walls are gypsum drywall, finished with a plaster-like surface, which Donna imprinted with branding irons, ropes, and horseshoes. Undaunted by her lack of experience, she said, "I didn't know what I was doing. I just got drywall mud and started slopping it on." She split old fence rails, which now support a wainscot-height wooden shelf for her many family photos and mementos. The bookshelves she built sag slightly and not all of the boards are cut evenly, but Donna is more delighted than disconcerted by these conditions. "I can't measure. I just go at it."

Unlike many of the homes and retreats around Cody, the room is not furnished with high-style western art and Molesworth-style furniture. Donna's taste is for used pieces obtained at secondhand stores and flea markets. Inventive uses are made of recycled materials such as the old red wagon seat that greets guests outside the entry. Inside her retreat space the focus is on the "genealogy wall"—on family, not possessions. Family roots are represented by one wall full of photographs of ancestral home places and kinfolk, flowing from the distant past right up to the present. Also proudly displayed is a needlepoint piece showing the history of Donna's Wyoming accomplishments, with scenes of reclaiming pasture lands from rocks, sage, and cactus, and the filling of badger and prairie dog

holes. In true form, she framed it herself, and the piece won blue ribbons in both the county and state fairs.

From building fence, to raising Scotch Highlander cattle, to filling gopher holes, Donna Johnson has had her creative hand in every crevice of her domain. She derives meaning from the doing of her multitude of projects and energy from the wide-open space of the countryside. Every move is made with thought and care, but nothing is precious because she knows that a new day will bring opportunities for fresh masterpieces. She works at it each day from six in the morning until nine at night and says, "Half the fun is thinking about it and half the fun is getting to it. . . . This place is my world and I thank God every day for being here."

When asked about advice for would-be retreat makers, Donna replied, "A lot of people talk about doing something different in their lives, but they never do it. Wally and I are very conservative and very thoughtful, yet here we are—out in the wild."

Operating outside of traditional mental models about hammers and saws, Donna Johnson's ongoing work of art brings her personal pleasure and renewal, as well as delight to those who are fortunate enough to know her.

Restacked logs from an old outbuilding serve as the perimeter for an outdoor cookhouse and family gathering place. The cookhouse— a project in progress— houses an eclectic collection of cooking devices, outdoor furniture, and Wally's bar clock that finally found a proper home.

TAR PAPER SHACK

People who like this sort of thing, will find this the sort of thing they like.

ABRAHAM LINCOLN

The Tar Paper Shack is comprised of a shed-roofed main space with additional plug-ons for bedroom, bathroom, utilities, and screened porch. Each is sheathed with a different color of tar paper.

OVER THE COURSE of his prosperous career, the man who started one of America's most successful franchise operations has always had a passion for envisioning, planning, and building. Tom Monaghan, president and CEO of Domino's Pizza, has built corporate headquarters buildings, an antique car museum, a Frank Lloyd Wright museum, and a luxurious corporate retreat on Drummond Island in northern Michigan. But the project that has brought him the most pleasure and satisfaction is the one he refers to simply as The Tar Paper Shack.

"I don't think I've had more fun doing anything than I had planning this thing." As he was starting to really enjoy the company of his five-year-old grandson Matthew, they dreamed together about the possibility of building a tree house on some secluded property about five minutes away from Monaghan's office. When it came right down to it, they hit on the scheme of building their "tree house" on the ground.

A galvanized metal tabletop surrounded by assorted and purposely mismatched chairs. Bunk beds for guests surround the living space, with a children's play loft above.

An ordinary, freestanding woodstove provides warmth and cheer on cold Michigan nights. Extra storage is gained by hanging chairs and games on the wooden wall framing.

Tom and Matthew sketched out their ideas on a yellow legal pad. Then came the tougher job of convincing architects and builders that all they really wanted was just a simple rectangular structure covered with tar paper. "Contractors couldn't believe that we were going to leave that tar paper on the outside," said Monaghan.

His architect said to him, "All of the time my clients are telling me they want things to look better, and you're telling me you want them to look worse." A legacy of financial success comes with its own set of complications.

Monaghan drew on the inspiration of a simple house that might have been built nearby long ago. "The theme we devised was that a crusty old bachelor built this place in the twenties, lived there all by himself until he died in 1949, then it sat empty until 1994. Then we came along, walked in, and it's just the way it was. I wanted it to be something that was really humble, like

the one this old bachelor would have built."

Though accustomed to working with some of the world's most talented architects and designers, on this project Monaghan and his grandson were the designers and interior decorators. Monaghan has long been a collector of fine antique furniture, but those heirlooms have no place of honor in this retreat. He went to antique shows with an entirely new perspective. He was searching for things that invoked nostalgic memories of his own childhood—a certain kind of dish, a particular style of salt-and-pepper shaker, some old pictures that seemed familiar. Drinking glasses at the retreat resemble the ones he used to wash as a soda jerk in high school.

The idea of a fireplace was rejected as being too showy, so a simple woodstove was used instead.

The central space is anchored by a large table with a galvanized metal top and surrounded by a dozen or so mismatched chairs. In fact, great care was taken to make sure they didn't match. The white-enameled electric stove and refrigerator are both from a bygone era. "I enjoyed going around with my grandson to flea markets, to junkyards, and to war surplus stores looking for stuff to furnish this place."

When asked the purpose of his retreat, Monaghan said it is first a place for his children, his seven grandchildren, and for family gatherings. They celebrate the opening day of

A timeworn stove, sink, and refrigerator could have been present in Monaghan's imaginary bachelor's shack.

Monaghan's bedroom is supported by a boulder, and the single window is positioned over his desk.

Industrial lighting, worn chairs, wood walls and ceilings, and telephone-pole structural columns give the cookshack the feeling of a medieval mead hall.

deer hunting season there, as well as Father's Day, and the Monaghan Men (and boys) have started a new family tradition of spending the night of December 23rd—Christmas Eve eve—at the shack. The patriarch and his grandson also go there nearly every Saturday after doing errands together. "We have some pretty adult kinds of conversations here. I sit here and say to myself, 'I can't believe this.' For Christmas I gave my grandson a key to the shack. These kids don't lack for presents, but this key is the thing he was most proud of. He keeps it in a special drawer at home. He is a partner with me."

However, the shack is not restricted only to family use. Its proximity to Domino's corporate headquarters has made it a natural choice for some company meetings and corporate entertaining. In fact, Monaghan indicates that he has not entertained in his home since he built this

place. He has hosted financial and industrial leaders and several Roman Catholic cardinals. All receive the same treatment—"lumberjack" shirts to wear during the day, and red flannel union suits for overnight stays—an exercise in contrasts.

Within Domino's, The Tar Paper Shack place has become almost legendary. Monaghan brings his top franchisees there to discuss company business and to give him recommendations in a relaxing atmosphere. He sums up the essence of the experience when he says, "I remember it started out with my grandson and doing sketches on a legal pad. Now here it is and people are enjoying it. That's kind of neat. I like creating those little moments of a smile and a surprise. This place always brings a smile to people's faces—always."

People experience personal retreat in many different ways. For some it is being in the place they have created, and for others it is the painstaking creation of long-contemplated plans. Monaghan seems to derive the most pleasure and renewal from the process of planning. From private schools to chapels to a major corporate empire, Monaghan is always building something. "The planning of things, for me, is as

much fun as having them."

Even in its simplicity, his planning zeal is still evident at The Tar Paper Shack. He has planned and constructed other structures on the same site. A cookshack, several wall tents on wooden platforms, and a miniature chapel are built. He is planning a sauna, a hot tub, and a tree house. Even another shack is being considered, with aged lumber instead of new 2 x 4s on the inside. "I plan on building another one and making this the bunkhouse. I want to make it more 'shack-ey' than this one."

When asked about his philosophy of retreat, Monaghan was consistent. "I'm kind of strange, I guess. I enjoy visualizing things and then building them. I really do enjoy bringing something about that wasn't there before." This is linked in some way to his approach as he continues to search for the meaningful things in life. "I suppose one way to find meaning in life is to go after what you think has meaning to find out whether it does or not. Frequently you find out that it doesn't, and so maybe that steers you toward what does. I certainly went through that before I built anything, in my daydreaming as a youngster. I created the greatest sand castles and realized that that wasn't important. Other things were more important, like why we are here and the hereafter."

So, has The Tar Paper Shack been a successful retreat for Monaghan? As a place for meditation and reflection, probably not completely. It is just too close to the everyday action. "I probably could be contemplative here if I couldn't be back in my office in five minutes and my home in seven or eight minutes." As a reminder of his youth and his roots it comes closer. "I spent a lot of my youth in upper Michigan. There are a lot of tar paper shacks up there with just a bed, a little table, and not much else." But as projects go, it has provided a great release and an outlet for his insatiable desire to plan and create.

And then there is perhaps the best benefit of all: "I just have a lot of fun with my grandson."

This miniature chapel is another of Monaghan's retreats on the property.

Tom Monaghan relaxes in the standard garb of guests at The Tar Paper Shack.

TIPI BY THE RIVER

Paradise is where I am.

VOLTAIRE

"I CALL MYSELF a tree translator," says Diane Cole, who is a rustic furniture designer and builder by trade. Though she operates without a fax machine, e-mail, Website, or other trappings of a traditional desk job, she still leads a sometimes hectic life as a single parent with a house in town, horses, dogs, kids, and a flourishing business to run.

Cole wasn't really looking to create a retreat, own a tipi, or even buy a piece of property. She was just earnestly searching for a way to remember and honor her deceased son, Simon. Several years ago, at the encouragement of a friend, she visited the land she now owns on the banks of the Jefferson River, just north of Willow Creek, Montana. Now her eighty acres, called the Climbing Simon Ranch, is home to a Sioux-style tipi, a tree house under construction, and an old barn that may someday become a studio. But mostly, the land is an undisturbed wild place that is home to turkeys, pelicans, skunks, herons, deer, hawks, porcupines, and cranes.

Cole's tipi is placed on the site with the entrance oriented to the east in order to capture the rays of the rising sun. The 16'-diameter tipi encloses just over 200 square feet, but its circular form makes it seem much larger.

Diane Cole creates one-of-a-kind pieces of furniture art. Her translation of these former trees became a rustic chair.

PHOTO © 1997 RIKSHOTS PHOTOGRAPHY

Sitting on a log by the Jefferson River, Diane Cole explains what it means to be a "tree translator."

Cole uses her retreat as a gathering place for friends, a family place for her sons, a place of reflection, and a place to remember Simon.

"The intent from the beginning was never to do anything to alter what this place is. I wanted it to really reflect who Simon was. He was a really free spirit." Her oldest son, Jason, is building a tree house, and her youngest son, Mac, comes out to fish and to drive around on their aging red tractor. She has no plans to get too carried away making her place something that it is not. It is wild and beautiful, and that is why she loves it.

The Climbing Simon is a place for her to set her consuming responsibilities temporarily aside and center herself. "The idea of retreat out here is to empty out, to make room for recognition of how the world really is as opposed to this false thing we create with deadlines and commitments, agendas, money, and 'stuff.' It requires some quiet time to really make room, to put your life in perspective, your place in the world in perspective. That's what this place does. It

reminds you of your place in the whole greater scheme of things."

For Cole, retreat has never been about a building. She recalls childhood fantasies of living in a rock cave in the Southwest desert or in a little lichen-covered house next to a stream but never in a house or a building. Her desire to be completely in a natural environment has led her to a lifelong love of tipis. While she had collected Indian dolls and miniature tipis as a child, her first real tipi came as a gift from the grandparents of a young man she helped through some tough times during a major scrape with the law. "He was a good kid—a little wild, but I can relate to that." That family tipi was a gift of love and became the first shelter on her land.

Tipi structures are able to withstand tremendous wind, rain, snow, and most of what nature has to offer. They aren't, however, designed to house cattle, so when the neighbor's cows paid an unexpected call, this first tipi was reduced to a set of wooden poles and strips of shredded canvas.

Now, Cole's "home on the land" is a new 16'-diameter tipi made by Don Ellis of White Buffalo Lodges in Livingston, Montana. "They haven't designed a tent yet which is as comfortable as a tipi," says Ellis. Both practical and beautiful, the conical structures are low-cost, easy to pitch, roomy, and well-lighted. They produce their own natural ventilation and thus are cool in the summer and provide a natural draft for a cozy winter fire.

Cole's tipi is carefully placed upon the earth with the entrance oriented in the time-honored eastern direction in order to capture the life-giving rays of the morning sun. "I walked around a long time out here before I put it in that spot," said Cole. "Retreat is really not in your head; it's in your heart. But maybe we just finally tune in to where it is and we begin to open up to it, and place becomes another thing that opens the door a little bit."

For Cole, there is meaning in the simple form, in the decor, and in the location. "A tipi is circular for a definite reason. There is something that goes on there." Her tipi is decorated with a combination of her own handcrafted furniture and traditional Native American items.

On the day this tipi was first erected, it was blessed by Cole's friend Tyler Medicine Horse, a member of the Crow tribe who is an artist in Bozeman and a Crow medicine man. "I understand how native or tribal people built symbolism and tradition and ritual and ceremony into

An interior tipi liner being installed. The liner keeps the critters out, provides insulation, and helps create the conditions for a natural draft to draw campfire smoke up and out.

their lives, because it is an ordering of their place and our place in the world," Cole explained. "You sit out here at night and look at the stars and you don't have the sense of being a very supreme entity; just a part if it all, which is really nice."

Diane Cole has fashioned a powerful and beautiful retreat without carving roads, reshaping the landscape, or building a trophy house. She is the caretaker of a place that replenishes her energy and feeds her soul. "Being out like this, and being where it is pretty simple, you don't have the distractions of life. You get to recognize that it is a circle. It's life and death and birth, life and death and birth. You see it in the seasons, and you see it in the things that live and die out here and return to the earth. There is some peace about that, and that's what living simply or going to a retreat is all about. It's kind of reconnecting with the really basic facts of life. We get so far away from that."

Cole's old barn, shelter for wandering neighbor cows, may someday become her studio.

Cole's tipi, decorated for its blessing ceremony with traditional Native American items, is now furnished with a combination of these things and her own handcrafted furniture.

WILSON WYOMING WOMEN

You know you've achieved
perfection in design,
Not when you have
nothing more to add,
But when you have
nothing more to take away.

ANTOINE DE SAINT-EXUPERY

Huidekoper's cabin was built from logs harvested from her own property.

I T WAS NO SURPRISE to discover a group of women artists living in the West who carry on the traditions of self-reliance, adventure, and capableness established long ago by their pioneer forebears. History has trained us to conjure these characteristics when we think of strong western women who have chosen unique lifestyles.

Three such women—all living in Wilson, Wyoming, near Jackson Hole—have developed lifestyles that center around personally shaped retreat environments.

Virginia Huidekoper lovingly repairs violins for local children in her upstairs retreat.

Georgie Morgan, Greta Gretzinger, and Virginia Huidekoper are neighbors. Their art forms are different—Morgan is a painter, Huidekoper is a writer and photographer, and Gretzinger is a muralist, illustrator, and graphic artist—but they seem to share some of those close-knit values borne out of living in a small town in a sometimes harsh northern climate. Their circumstances have shaped them as people, and through their artistic and community expression, they have shaped the situation around them.

They have another similarity. All have retreat places that fall outside the normal definition.

• • •

Virginia Huidekoper believes that people should change directions or "reinvent" them-selves every seven years. She seems to have been a faithful follower of her own advice. A map on her log cabin wall is filled with brightly colored pins designating all of the cities and towns across America she visited as the avid pilot of a single engine airplane. She had visited the Jackson Hole area in the late 1930s to ski, and in 1943 she and her new husband, Jim, had made it their permanent home.

"We took a year off from college to climb and ski, and the year is still going on." With her mountaineering husband she climbed all of the principal peaks in the range, and she skied hard for many years. Her skiing pursuits have slowed a bit in the last several years, but she proclaims it is because of waning interest, not waning ability.

Crowded with hand tools, power tools, and mementos from her past, Huidekoper's retreat is a place where she puts her love for community into action.

"The first fifty years of anything are the best," she says.

As a writer, photographer, and newspaper woman, she has chronicled the current events and history of Jackson Hole for over fifty years. Soon after moving to the area, she and her husband bought the local newspaper, the *Jackson Hole Courier.* "I've always been interested in newspapers—the typography, design, layout, the whole bit. In 1970 the local paper was terrible, so a friend and I talked about it and decided to start another paper. We just went ahead and ordered the machinery and started in." Thus was born the still-thriving *Jackson Hole News.* She and her partner did everything from writing the news to taking the photographs to folding the printed papers. "It was fun. We had a great crew of young people and a great spirit."

Huidekoper's log cabin home was constructed in 1975, built from logs taken from her own property. She built the cabin with assistance from local craftsmen and ski bums trying to support their habits. "All of the folks who did the chinking were dopers. You had to be to do chinking."

Though her somewhat remote cabin home is in itself retreat-like, Huidekoper has a special place within the cabin she uses for personal restoration—restoration of her spirit and restoration of violins for children in the local community orchestra. Many consider a wood shop to be just that—a shop. And most assume that such a place belongs in the garage or, at the very least, in the basement. Huidekoper has chosen to put her shop in a place of honor on the second floor of her small home. A room with a view. Two mice played while she showed and talked about violins in various states of repair as well as two antique wooden clamps that she discovered as display window props in San Francisco. "You just can't buy them like that anymore—and I got them for only $5 each!"

Huidekoper has always been interested in musical instruments. "I've always been building

things since I was five years old. In the 1930s, Wanda Landowski was the foremost harpsichordist in the country, and I had one of her recordings. I read on the record jacket that she had built a harpsichord, and ever since then I had wanted to build one." When her oldest daughter, Christie, was in school, she was playing a spinet (a small harpsichord with a single keyboard). Huidekoper decided she needed a better musical instrument, so she built the first harpsichord, which she proclaims to be a "simple deal." After that, her other daughter, Zaidee, an accomplished cellist and music teacher, inspired her to build another. After being in touch with Frank Hubbard, the foremost authority on harpsichords in the country, she combined a kit of basic hardware with wood from the local lumberyard to make a beautiful French double-manual instrument. "It is a significant instrument, with two keyboards, three sets of strings and all of that."

Along the way she has also built a guitar—"something to do instead of playing bridge"—and a clavichord—"they are not worth bothering with; you can't hear them. As a little boy, Handel practiced in the attic and his family didn't know. I can believe it!"

Huidekoper's instrument-building activities so inspired the daughter of her good friend Georgie Morgan that the younger Morgan went away to school to learn the craft of making fine harpsichords. Said Georgie, "In a little community like this one, we all inspire each other." To which Virginia replied, "We're neighbors!"

Huidekoper's retreat is dusty and cluttered. It is not filled with fine furniture or great art. It is filled with memories of the past and worthwhile projects for the future, with love and caring and a neighborly attitude that seems to reflect an accurate picture of the person who inhabits it.

• • •

Georgie Morgan didn't set out to build a personal retreat but rather was investigating a way to help her neighbors—neighbors she didn't

The 10' x 12' straw-bale structure uses a post-and-beam construction method to hold up the wood-framed roof. Straw bales are used for infill between the corners and are finished with an interior and exterior plaster.

Georgie Morgan inside her straw-bale shed retreat.

Interior of the shed
showing wooden roof
framing, metal roof,
sculptural windows, and
a "cornerstone"
inscribed with the year
of completion.

even know yet. At a yoga class she took with Libby Crews Wood, executive director of the Snake River Institute, she learned that the institute was interested in exploring some alternative construction methods and new approaches to affordable, low-cost housing for workers in Wilson, a close-knit Wyoming community beginning to burst at the seams from an influx of well-to-do transplants building spacious homes. The institute brings together groups of people to celebrate western traditions and to explore issues facing the contemporary West. In this case, they wanted to demonstrate that straw-bale construction would be a practical approach to solving a community dilemma. When Georgie and her husband John learned that the group needed a place to construct a bale-house prototype, they offered some room on their family ranch.

Several factors about straw-bale housing attracted them—ease and simplicity of construction, ready availability and affordability of materials, environmental sensibility, and the community spirit that might be generated by the "barn raising" approach to such a project.

There was one catch for the group, however: Wyoming building officials weren't familiar with this type of construction and weren't yet convinced of its long-term structural viability. Thus they denied Morgan's band of builders a permit for a habitable structure. Not to be dissuaded from investigating this building type, Morgan and company decided to build a garden shed as a test structure. Says Morgan, "We wanted to prove to the building official that it was a viable kind of building material."

A site was selected and a date was set for a four-day "workshop" to be led by Bill and Athena Steen, authors of the bale construction bible, *The Straw Bale House.*

A straw-bale building is built by carefully stacking bales of compacted, dry, organic waste material—wheat straw, rice straw, corn husks,

bean stalks, or grass. Says Athena Steen, "You want to use what is trash, not good animal feed. You can use whatever, as long as it's dry and not worth a lot." The bales are anchored to the ground and to each other with steel reinforcing rods. The structure can be roofed with a variety of traditional or nontraditional systems, and the walls can be finished inside and out with a number of different plaster and stucco variations.

All things considered, straw bales literally stack up as a remarkable building material. They are produced from a waste product that can be sustainably grown in a short period of time, are biodegradable, and can help alleviate multiple environmental problems with their use. They are easy to modify, flexible enough to be used in a variety of ways, solid and substantial, durable over time, and easy to maintain. In addition, they require only inexpensive, uncomplicated tools and unspecialized labor, and are easily acquired and affordable in most locations around the world. (From *The Straw Bale House* by Steen, Steen and Bainbridge, Chelsea Green Publishing Company, 1994, p. 21.)

When complete, these buildings are energy-efficient, fire-resistant, and earthquake-resistant. Similar construction systems have been used to build simple houses in Mexico for as little as $300 each.

Straw-bale construction lends itself to inventive sculptural elements that can be introduced by the creators during construction.

A customary "truth window" verifies that the walls are indeed straw.

The 10' x 12' structure was built by a dozen or so people over four days. The result of their efforts is a delightful organic structure that, for naming purposes, has been deemed a "garden shed." It can't be called an "artist's studio," because that would make it a habitable structure and contrary to the building code, so Georgie uses it as a home for her clay pots and gardening implements, and to take an occasional creative respite from the work they represent. A garden retreat.

Says Steen, "It was fun watching how people can't just build a shed. It starts dawning on them, and they go 'wow, we can't use this as a storage shed. It's too nice.' They start introducing really nice elements into it—sculpturally or as little doors or windows. People start really contributing to it. You really get a nice coming-together energy."

Garden shed or not, the building was built with love and is beautifully detailed. "There is something aesthetically beautiful about all of the handwork," says Georgie Morgan. John Morgan summed it up as he commented on the ease of the construction and the community that can participate: "Grandmothers and children can do the work."

• • •

"It was cheap. That was the number one thing. It was being sold cheap and I bought it," says **Greta Gretzinger** of the 280-square-foot (8' x 35') trailer house that has been art studio and home to her for the last thirteen years. A simple trailer house, yes—but a usual trailer house, absolutely not. Located along the road to a ritzy ski village north of Jackson Hole, the Rancho Flamingo is a witty counterpoint to the exclusive golf course across the street.

Gretzinger has taken a fun-loving, retreat-like approach to her full-time living and working situation. Her place is small, doesn't require much maintenance, and certainly doesn't take itself too seriously. A few years ago when her trailer needed painting, she decided to transform it into

Wooden corner columns support the roof. The spaces between the wood are stuffed with straw and plastered differently to add interest and definition to the corners.

An exterior wall next to the door is signed by the artists who built it.

Greta Gretzinger works in her studio, surrounded by her collection of collections.

a log home. "I like the whole idea that it's a log house—that I've got a log house in Jackson Hole." And while she was at it, she decided to bring someone else into her life. "When I was painting my house, I decided I may as well paint myself a husband at the same time. That's when I painted Elvis."

As a muralist, Gretzinger has had occasions to work in the large "trophy houses" that are being built all around the Jackson Hole area. Her interactions with some people have caused her to wonder about their understanding of the area, and what they are really searching for. "For some, their house is dead. It looks like something out of a catalog and you wonder what the attraction is for them. A lot of the people who have come here lately like to look at [the area]

but don't know what else to do with it."

As she compares her tiny abode to those of her neighbors, does she wish for a larger space? "I don't covet other people's houses, but I do covet their garages. I only feel envious when I look at some big garage and think what I could do there."

Because of the size of her studio space and the "artifacts" she collects, Gretzinger is sometimes limited to smaller paintings than she would prefer. "The good thing is that I can't collect too much junk, and the bad thing is I can't collect too much junk. If I had more room, I'd probably be just like a goldfish: I'd grow into whatever space I had, and it would be just as cluttered. I could see myself living in a space this small forever."

Gretzinger's many props, trophies, and treasures are displayed and stored on every surface of her small abode.

So as to blend in with the view, the rear of the Rancho Flamingo is painted to match the mountains.

So what and where is retreat for a woman who lives in a space smaller than the dressing rooms in many of the local castles? Every fall she packs up her Subaru with Mona Lisa painted on the hood and takes a three-week trip through the Southwest. Her car is her calling card, her hotel, and her retreat while on the road. "I retreat from all the marvelous luxury of this place, and then I come back in the winter and I've got hot water and a stove, and it seems big again. It would be like someone who had a real house going to a cabin. It serves the same purpose. It gives me perspective on what I really need and what are luxuries and how nice it is to have the things that I do have and to come back and feel like this place is more spacious than I would normally think if I hadn't left to see other places."

Retreat is where you find it—if you know where and how to look.

Gretzinger's painted husband keeps watch over the ranch

For three weeks each autumn, this car becomes a retreat for Greta Gretzinger. The personalized Mona Lisa assures that Gretzinger will attract conversation wherever she goes.

THE HOUSES THAT BAIRD BUILT

*To travel hopefully
is a better thing than to arrive,
and the true success is to labour.*

ROBERT LOUIS STEVENSON

Builder Terry Baird and interior designer Hillary Heminway collaborated to convert a well-used sheep wagon into this cozy, self-contained, mobile retreat.

"HOUSE BUILDING is building boxes. Furniture building is building boxes. A house is nothing more than a bigger box," or so says Terry Baird, a Montanan who has made a career of crafting beautiful boxes both small and large.

Thirty years ago Baird was a bored high-school senior who was lucky enough to find a subject that inspired him and a great teacher who planted some seeds that have been growing and flourishing ever since. Somewhere along the way, Terry's dad gave him a book entitled *Early American Pine Furniture*. A good wood shop teacher, a pile of discarded crate lumber, and an insightful gift set him on a lifelong journey of building—both experience and things.

Early on, Baird constructed simple "country" furniture that he sold for beer money, but soon his innate desire to learn, to grow, and to stretch

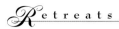

took over. "I bought a set of plans for a grand-mother's clock. I thought that would be impossible to build, but I built this clock. It looked nice, and it wasn't impossible. I felt like I had just gotten to the top of Mt. Everest, but I found myself asking, 'So what do I do next?'"

After high school, Baird left Minnesota and moved with his family to the small ranching town of Big Timber, Montana. Soon after beginning to pursue a teaching degree at Montana State University, he realized that what really brought him satisfaction was making things with his own hands. After one year he left MSU and decided to transfer to the University of Experience. He picked up and moved to the growing oil boom-town of Casper, Wyoming. "I had just enough experience to feel halfway competent. I hit town, hopped in my pickup, and drove around to the job sites. I got on with this guy who framed houses. I had a carpentry book called *Modern Carpentry,* and at night I'd study that book so when I went to the job the next day, I'd know what was going on." After two years and many tract houses, the job got boring. So it was back to Big Timber for Terry and his wife, Jill, and on to the next phase of his box-building odyssey.

"Doing log cabins was really a new curve for me. I thought you had to be a mastermind to build one, but I found it was like throwing a diamond hitch on a packhorse—you get a book, read about it, practice a little bit, and boom, you can throw a diamond!"

Baird rapidly gained experience and a reputation for reclaiming and renovating fine log cabins in southwest Montana. Because of his inquisitive approach, every job would lead to some new understanding of how to do things differently or better. He learned from his clients, from his crew, and by making mistakes. "You have to taste it. You never learn anything but by making mistakes." All of the experiences he gathered were carefully filtered over time and have become a part of his personal style and philosophy of building.

He noticed that when most people built or renovated a log house, they used materials they could get at the local lumberyard, such as aluminum-clad windows and hollow-core wooden doors. Says Baird, "Using off-the-shelf stuff on an old log building is kind of like having a Model T Ford and making it into a hot rod. It looks cool, but it just ain't what you were shooting for." Instead he scrounges materials from dilapidated barns and old homestead sites. He has swapped for or bought ancient log buildings that may still wait for years until he finds just the right use or new owner for the antique materials. "In America people have been brainwashed into thinking new is better. We live in a throw-away society. I like to find the old materials and put them back. It's a way of recycling that people don't even think about, and at the same time it is saving a little bit of history."

Baird's individual style and high level of artistic craftsmanship have led to his being one of the most sought-after builders of homes and retreat places in the Boulder River valley. "Initially I just figured I was making the car payment and putting beans on the table," he says. "All of a sudden I realized that I've put together a talent over twenty years, and it's been fun. Instead of just assembling someone's house, it is a lot more fun to put together a project that is really personal, unique, and classy."

His reputation eventually brought him clients such as TV news anchor Tom Brokaw, fashion photographer Bruce Weber, actor Michael Keaton, Academy Award-winning composer Dave Grusin, and author Tom McGuane. For each of them, he has created retreat environments that make extensive use of old and recycled materials.

Success, however, bred its own complement of new frustrations for Baird. After waking up one day and realizing that a large crew and multiple projects were preventing him from doing what he really likes, he decided to make some changes. "I tried the big thing—that's the

PHOTO © 1997 AUDREY HALL

American way—bigger is better; more employees, you make more money. But you've got your neck on this chopping block with this ax just teetering there. I can understand why executives in big corporations jump out of windows. The reason I like construction is because I like hands-on work—nailing two boards together and making them look good."

Just as he had about decided to quit building altogether, interior designer Hillary Heminway showed up on his doorstep. She had an idea about taking old sheep wagons and converting them into tiny but exquisite retreat "cabins." Montana Wagons was born and Baird turned his

energies from building large homes to self-contained living environments that are less than 100 square feet in size and are made like fine pieces of furniture. He has evolved from a furniture builder, to a house builder, to a craftsman who builds houses like furniture, to an artisan who builds furniture that is a house.

Baird credits Heminway with the initial sheep wagon idea but is willing to admit that he added something to it. "I'm not an original idea man," he says. "I'm the kind of guy who can see something and kind of modify it. Everybody learns that way. That's why artists go to Europe to study the great masters."

A full-size double bed with storage beneath occupies one end of the sheep-wagon retreat.

In addition to meeting the utilitarian needs for cooking, the wagon kitchen area is equipped with carefully chosen utensils that contribute to the overall ambience of the space.

Baird opens the cabin for use by removing the wooden panels that protect it from wandering bears and curious trespassers. The minimal tools necessary for opening and closing the cabin are stored behind a removable panel under the porch.

Finally, after twenty-some years of making retreat places sing for others, Baird has composed a little melody for himself. His first step was finding an ideal place to build. With a partner he purchased 150 acres known around his valley as "the old sawmill place." It overlooks the main Boulder River and has a view up the East Boulder drainage, where Baird lives. The property is accessible only by foot, four-wheeler, snowshoe, snowmobile, or horseback.

It took Baird and two other carpenters about a week to construct the 12' x 16' cabin in Baird's garage. They built it as a kit, took it apart, hauled it to the site, and screwed it back together. The cabin spent its first several seasons with only a tar-paper covering over the wood-plank walls, but recently Baird swapped some "hunting camp time" for a friend's help in putting on the exterior wood siding. The rectangular space accommodates two folding cots, a small table and several chairs, and a woodstove. Sixteen-penny nails serve as hangers for pans, saws, hats, and blankets. When the cabin is not in use, the door and window openings are covered with screwed-on panels to protect it from animals and overly inquisitive

The cabin was built in stages and spent several seasons covered only with tar paper over the wood plank walls.

hikers. A hidden-away ratchet screwdriver acts as the exterior locking system. Without electricity or plumbing, lighting is by candle and gasoline lantern. Fresh water comes to an outdoor sink in black plastic pipe, gravity-fed from a small spring a hundred feet up the mountain, and a traditional outhouse serves as the sanitary sewer.

A simple rectangular form, ordinary construction methods, and the most basic of interior furnishings combine to make for a princely hideaway. Baird muses, "That's what everybody is trying to escape to. We all love the modern life and all of its conveniences, but our hearts really lie out here. We're related to prehistoric crea-

The simple 12' x 16' space accommodates cooking, dining, sleeping, and gear storage. A vaulted ceiling makes the space feel generous.

Fresh water is gravity-fed to a sink outside, and this outhouse is the sanitary sewer system.

With no electricity, the heating, cooking, and lighting are fueled with wood, kerosene, and propane.

The cabin, safely buttoned up, will rest until Baird's next visit.

tures, you know, and my sense is that everybody needs fresh air. In a society where you are in your car, there are police, and where the roads are plowed, after a snow you feel secure because there are other people around, even though you are afraid someone is going to slit your throat, steal your car, or burn your house down. But it's different to get somewhere where it is just you— one-on-one with Nature. It's nice to build a little shack you can walk or snowshoe in to. You arrive under your own power. When you go there, there is nothing better."

• • •

Having helped dozens of others plan their retreats, Baird has some advice for those who may be contemplating a place of their own. It boils down to dreaming, planning, and taking things one step at a time.

He suggests starting with a dream. "If you want a retreat, it is something you should dream about for a while. I've noticed that some people have as much fun dreaming about their retreat as they do having it." He believes that if you have a strong enough dream and combine it with a written plan and some goals, you can get where you are aiming.

About carrying out the plan, he suggests a gradual approach, with plenty of time for test experiences and reflection along the way. "You don't need to go to an outdoor equipment store and buy all of this fancy equipment. You might consider making your stuff. That's part of your retreat; your relaxation; the soothing, healthy part of the whole deal. Your temporary retreat could be a wall tent set up on United States Forest Service land, which, as an American, you already own. You can stay there for fourteen days every year."* Baird prefers to take short, well-considered steps instead of quick, long strides. Sitting on a wooden folding chair at his cabin table and looking out over the mountains, Baird summarized, "It might take ten years, but you can manage that, and in the process of getting there you learn so much about yourself."

* Baird is referring to National Forest System land, which is administered by the Forest Service. Regulations are different from one national forest to another, so it's a good idea to check with a local Forest Service office for variations.

On the front porch of his cabin, Terry Baird takes the time to dream and plan—for himself and for others.

MUSINGS ON ZUNI

Fortunate too is the man who has come to know the gods of the countryside.

VIRGIL

The Zuni retreat after years of sanding, scraping, painting, fixing, and loving.

THE ONLY ZUNIS I knew about were the Pueblo people in western New Mexico and the exquisitely carved fetishes my wife and I have collected for a number of years. I certainly wasn't searching for a retreat in Zuni, Virginia, when I became acquainted with Deborah Marquardt. I had never even heard of Zuni, though I have lived in Virginia all my life.

The first time we met in person we were both doing some work for a company that was holding an off-site symposium at a rural retreat center near Wakefield, Virginia, which, by chance, happens to be near Zuni. Our rapport quickly flourished and our conversations turned to our other projects, which included my book on retreats. Deborah volunteered the information that she and her companion, Jim Raper, owned a retreat nearby and that it had in time become

Doing the work themselves was part of the retreat experience for Deborah and Jim. This screened porch is one of the additions they made to the original "little red house."

their permanent home but was soon to be sold due to their impending move to southern France. She invited me to have a look, and what I found was actually a collection of wonderful retreat places on a single property—an old shed, a small cottage, a swimming pool covered by a screened gazebo, gardens, and a brick bread oven.

My first exploration didn't last long, a half hour at most. We agreed upon a subsequent visit, a promised gourmet meal, long interviews, and perhaps an overnight stay. But summer schedules, family obligations, and the crisis-level activities surrounding an international move all conspired to prevent us from realizing our rendezvous. Thus Deborah and Jim escaped to France without my ever having an opportunity to more fully experience their retreat. So I sent along to France pages of questions, and several months after their move, I received these "musings on Zuni." What follows are their descriptions, reflections, and memories of this place in southern Virginia and a decade's worth of experiences there.

JIM'S MUSINGS ON ZUNI

Our little place in the woods at Zuni was a retreat long before I bought it. I was going through a divorce. I didn't have a lot of money to spend, yet I wanted several acres of property. I was looking for a peaceful place. The ad Deborah and I answered offered for sale a small house with acreage near Windsor. We went to see it right away. It was a cinder-block house and was a possibility. But what really grabbed my eye was the porch-red little wooden abode nearby. Unlike the cinder-block house, the wooden one was set back off the dirt lane that led down to the property. There was also the shed, which looked pretty junky but still seemed to have possibilities. I was as excited as a kid at Christmas. I dreamed all sorts of things for the property, even though we hadn't yet had the chance to inspect the house or shed or to walk the land.

One had to be a little dream-struck to appreciate the house. It was tiny and the interior was . . . well . . . a project. The two bedrooms had pockmarked and water-stained walls. The bathroom was dingy. And the great room didn't look so great, with its dark paneled walls, clashing blonde cabinets in the kitchen at one end, and great big cast-iron woodstove protruding from the blocked-off fireplace at the other end of the room. Even worse, the ceiling panels between the exposed rafters were nothing more than Styrofoam insulation, smoke-stained and haphazardly installed.

However, the fireplace mantel was handsome and in good shape. And all that exposed wood in the ceiling reminded me of a lodge in the mountains—the Alleghenies or even the Alps. We walked the property and found the two streams on the borders, the pond, and, back in the woods, the decrepit foundations for someone else's long-forgotten dream house. The site was overgrown with pines, but it would be fairly easy to clear and just the place, perhaps, for me to build my pet project—the "pool with screened porch over it." At least that is how the county would eventually describe it for building-permit and tax purposes.

I bought seven acres with the tiny red wooden house, the shed, and a couple of small pole barns. The property was shaped like a slice of pie, with streams, or runs, forming the long sides and a dirt lane as the third side.

With the cottage came the long, slope-roofed farm building that had been around for several decades before the other buildings. At one time, it had been nothing more than a tin roof held up by creosote-soaked uprights, forming seven or eight open bays where tractors and implements and tools could be protected from the elements. At some point someone had closed in three of the bays and poured a concrete floor to create an "apartment" and rec room.

The apartment had a bathroom of sorts (the urinal hung on the wall and drained into a

trench behind the building). The toilet flushed into a jury-rigged septic tank that was no more than an old oil drum with lime in it, punctured here and there so it could drain. There was room for a bed or two, and in the corner was a small kitchen.

The shed, as we called it, was a perfect retreat for those who wanted to enjoy the great outdoors, or, more likely, the great indoors. The rec room had a gorgeous old pool table in the middle of it, and along the walls were high-backed oak booths with seat cushions covered in red vinyl. The booths had been salvaged from a roadhouse somewhere and gave the place the look of a nip joint. There was even an old Pepsi thermometer, three feet square, hanging on the outer wall.

Looking back, I know we tried to do too much too soon. I hired construction workers without thoroughly checking references. One team wrecked the little red house, where I was allowing them to live for a few days while they began construction on the swimming pool

A hand-stacked outdoor bread oven was made from salvaged bricks bought for $20 at an auction down the road.

structure. Two other workers suddenly disappeared, and I found out later that they had last been seen in the custody of police. I hired a painter and roofer whose work habits were exasperating. About the only workers I could really count on were Deborah and myself and a few friends.

Six months it took to get the house and shed in decent order. Among the projects were spackling, painting inside and outside, new shingles for the roof, a new ceiling for the great room, removal of the woodstove and rehabilitation of the fireplace, refinishing of floors, new siding for the shed, more painting inside the shed, hauling junk, planting grass and flowers, and building raised vegetable gardens.

Meanwhile, work on the pool structure ground to a halt. I wanted so much for it to be ready for our first summer season, but nothing I did brought progress. The pool was installed, but the 26' x 42' gazebo-like building going up over it was only a skeleton through that summer. Without a roof over the pool and without proper electrical hookup for the pump/filter, the pool water got dirtier and dirtier, blossomed in algae, and stank. It would be a year and a half from the start of construction before we first splashed in the pool, and there were times during the construction nightmares that I was sure we never would. By the next summer we finally had a swimming pool, and the place became the "spa." Rather quickly its reputation as a retreat grew among family and friends.

At some point my love for the place went into high gear. I left my job at a large newspaper and moved full time to the country, took out the bunk beds in the one bedroom and created an office. I loved being alone out there during the days, writing. Every season was delightful. It was a place I could think. I even began to paint, at first on paper and then on canvases, and soon the house was a gallery for my work. An artist friend declared my paintings "primitive." I liked the description.

I bought four adjoining acres and thought I might build a "real" house out there someday. But plans were coming together for our long-dreamed-of year in France. Friends at first fell in line to rent the place while we were gone, but each of their schemes eventually fell through. We didn't trust just anybody to keep up the property, especially the pool. And somewhere deep inside us was the shared feeling that perhaps perfect retreats don't last forever. They might have a finite time to them. Perhaps we were ready for a new retreat. France would be one, but only for a year. Then we could come back, anxious, yes, but excited by the opportunity to create in another way and in another place a retreat as dear to us as the place in the country at Zuni.

DEBORAH'S MUSINGS ON ZUNI

I remember the first day we saw it—in the late fall. Leaves were crunchy under the feet, and the sun's shadows were weakening. Nestled in a stand of pines was a little red cottage, immediately compelling, even with its obvious blemishes. It was peaceful. You could feel your shoulders drop just standing there.

The inside of the house was a surprise. There were exposed beams in the ceiling, a nice hearth, and when no one was looking, I peeled back the corner of some linoleum to discover hardwood floors. Even though it was your basic one-story on the outside, inside there was more architectural interest than I would have guessed. At least enough to make up for the cheap paneling and paint. The little house seemed to cry out, "Fix me. Love me."

The first few months seemed like camping while we made the cottage livable on our terms. The ceiling had not been finished. We learned to cut drywall in contour to fit between the beams that had no even measure end to end. We cooked meals on a woodstove and peed in the woods.

We hauled junk. We bought new shingles for the roof and a picnic table for the yard. We

painted the house white and planted window boxes with bright red geraniums. It was hard work. Yet that first spring we caught a glimpse of what the place could be. A huge stand of wild azaleas erupted like popcorn—white, pink, and red. Elixir for tired bones.

Here, a day's work was a day's work. It felt good. We retreated from the office. This was not the kind of place to bring that kind of work. Admiring a finished project, we'd sip wine and

plan the next, expanding on our little dream. A white picket fence at the road, a pool table in the outbuilding. A swimming pool in the woods, a screened-in front porch. With every little project, the property returned bigger dividends. The place began to resemble an escape within an escape within an escape—like one of those old Russian dolls that you can take apart and find, in descending size, little copies of itself.

My biggest contribution was furnishings.

The great room is anchored by a large refectory table and a butcher-block table for food preparation. The white vaulted ceiling makes this relatively small space feel much larger than it actually is.

The great room is made comfortable by the original fireplace, Jim's paintings, and Deborah's collection of furniture salvaged from auctions, flea markets, and yard sales.

Again, there was no plan. I outfitted the place in found objects culled from auctions, flea markets, yard sales, and Maggie's shop down the lane. Call it adaptive reuse. A pie safe, stripped of seven layers of paint, housed our tiny stereo and a collection of Shawnee corn pottery. An iron bed, a Morris chair, wrought-iron porch furniture and antiques from wine making took their places. Even our kitten was someone else's discard, rescued from the side of the road at eleven days old, making this place his own as he grew up. The great room was anchored by a large refectory table and an old butcher block for food preparation. Everything had an assignment, like on a boat. If you made a mess in one place, you had to clean up before starting the next project, one of the advantages, I think, to a small living space.

Soon it was obvious: In the process of creating a retreat for ourselves, we had made one for friends as well. From the beginning, friends got a kick out of visiting. One couple couldn't believe we'd live down a potholed dirt lane, so they kept driving until they found new construction but never our mailbox. Another Manhattanite couldn't understand how we could possibly stand all the noise when a chorus of tree frogs—peepers—broke into song. Someone donated a hammock, which we slung between two trees. Someone else, a wooden swing. Another friend brought tools and installed speakers and a stereo at the pool, and another kept two beehives, from which we all enjoyed fresh honey. Some friends began calling it the "spa." Others begged to care for it when we traveled. We'd swim naked under the stars, escaping convention. Legends grew. Like the time a friend gigged 36 frogs in our pond and we dined on homemade biscuits and frog legs for breakfast. The time a copperhead showed up at a dinner party. The times Jim's youngest son organized paint-gun wars in the woods.

How or when a discussion of an outdoor bread oven began, I have no memory. It may have started with the pile of bricks I bought at auction for $20 the day they liquidated Maggie's estate. Some we used to lay paths in the herb garden. The rest we stacked neatly in the yard. Then one cold day in January, I arrived to the aroma of baking bread—outside. Jim had rearranged the bricks, covered the pile in good old Isle of Wight clay, and fashioned a French *boule,* which we devoured in no time. Another legend and many more loaves.

As the house evolved, so did we. Maybe in some ways this little place helped us realize what is important in life—a relationship, the land.

So it was from this retreat that we started planning our next one—a year in France. Retreats, after all, have more to do with spirit than space. You retreat from one thing to run toward something else. With that in mind, we retreated to the country house full time. We weren't finished in Zuni. It had to prepare us for France.

Jim quit his high-pressure job as managing editor of a 200,000-circulation newspaper to write a novel that had been simmering for twenty years. I continued to commute to a studio to maintain my freelance writing business. Each evening I took nourishment from the retreat. Evenings were bathed in conversation and planning. Sometimes Jim had a painting to show. He established himself as a wine columnist. I dabbled in *pique-assiette,* the art of making mosaic from broken pottery chards, and I refinished furniture in the shed. And we shaped our new dream into reality.

The house now belongs to a family with a different dream and vision. It is their "before" picture. As I followed Jim out of the driveway that last time, all our belongings in a rental truck en route to storage, I carried only the memories.

We were off to another adventure, tickets to France in hand. Open to all possibilities. Boarding the plane, we had packed one last lesson from the Zuni retreat: Making dreams come true is damned hard work, but it feels great!

Bright, airy, and rustic, the spa feels like the outdoors, but the pool is protected from leaves and trash, and swimmers from annoying insects.

The spa—a 26' x 42' screened gazebo covering the pool. Its translucent, corrugated, fiberglass roof allows maximum natural light during the day and on moonlit nights.

THE EXECUTIVE SUITE

*As no man is born an artist,
so no man is born an angler.*

IZAAK WALTON

MICHAEL NOUROT first spotted his future retreat on the back of a pickup truck in the San Francisco Bay area in 1969. By the early seventies, its original owner, who was studying glassmaking at Chico State, had grown tired of living in the home-built camper, and in a brilliant commercial property exchange, Nourot swapped three hand-blown glass plates (worth $700 at the time) for his haven. Thus was born—or adopted—The Executive Suite, as it has been known ever since.

At first, Nourot moved this freestanding pickup camper inside of his Benicia, California, studio as a place for Michael's wife and artist partner, Ann Corcoran, to get away for some time to herself while pregnant with their first child. They removed the existing sink and did a few other renovations, including installing a portable potty, to make the small room comfortable. Except for those minor changes, the space remains just as it was when they acquired it—

Essentially unchanged since it came off of its original pickup truck home, The Executive Suite is constructed of wood framing sheathed with painted plywood. The brightly colored spheres emit light into the small space.

Parked among the various accoutrements of the glassmaking operation, The Executive Suite is both convenient and removed.

Red Flash **large flute by Michael Nourot.**

complete with tie-dyed tapestry, hippie murals, and an oil painting by deceased California artist Harold Ball. In fact, the colorful period decor is one of Michael's favorite aspects. "It has the feeling that you are all rolled up in a Persian carpet."

After many years of service, the exterior is in need of a few repairs, but Nourot has never had the desire to change the interior. "I love it. Having grown up in San Francisco in the late sixties with all the smokin' and hootin' that was going on then, it suits me. I'd hate for anyone to think I'm normal."

Soon after their daughter's birth, Ann gave over the getaway to Michael, and now, except for an occasional visit by a fly-fishing cohort, it is used almost exclusively by him. "About that time I had gotten pretty seriously into fly-fishing, and so I started using it as my fly-tying shop because it gave me a chance to get away from my work and go into my little fantasy 'I'm going to catch a fish' world."

Monday through Thursday of each week, Michael and Ann, along with their partner, David Lindsay, are busy making and blowing some of the finest decorative glass in America. Making glass at this level is a highly creative and physically challenging art form. Though basic design ideas can be formed in advance, molten glass sometimes creates magic of its own, so its human helpers have to be totally tuned in to their work in order to assist in the enchanting results. It requires focus and total concentration, it's hot and somewhat dangerous, and blowing glass is just plain hard work!

"I make a lot of glass. I make a lot of glass because I love making glass," says Nourot, but in order to freshen himself and his creative spirit, he needs to get away from it as well. "It's impossible to sit here at my desk and think, because people are asking questions all the time or they are wondering what I am doing just staring out of the window." Off to The Executive Suite.

Nourot's retreat is now located just outside the door of the Nourot • Corcoran • Lindsay Glass Studio and gallery. He finds some time every day to spend there—to rest, to think, to reflect, and to rejuvenate. "I use it every day from fifteen minutes to a couple of hours, depending on what is going on that day. I spend a lot of time thinking about my glass out there. That's one of the things that is important to me—what I'm going to do the next day, or what I did today, or how I'm going to set up a month-long campaign in order to get all the different things done I promised for people." Nourot says that in his fly-tying shop is where most of his mental creativity takes place, where he imagines new glass patterns or designs that eventually find expression through his eyes and hands in the raw glass and finished glassware.

He also uses The Executive Suite as a place to unwind and center himself before he leaves

PHOTO © 1997 LAWSON DRINKARD

for home each evening. "Almost always after I have finished my day, I go out there to sort of cool down before I go home. Sometimes I have thought that if I moved the fly shop home, then I'd get more time to tie flies, but then I've realized it's at exactly the right spot."

The Executive Suite is a very small space—less than fifty square feet—but for Nourot, that is part of what is special to him. His fly-tying bench, materials, books, and other anchors of

Fur, feathers, tinsel, and thread are the makings of flies that will attract the cunning trout. Nourot's tying bench envelops him when he is in his retreat.

Michael Nourot finishes a piece of glass.

and intimate—all traits of successful retreats.

So what is it about tying flies that provides retreat experience for Nourot? In contrast to the necessity of working quickly with 2,000-degree molten glass, the hooks and fur and feathers used to tie artificial trout flies allow a more patient and reflective approach to a task. And, in order to tie the most effective flies, he must mentally put himself on the banks of the stream, or even under the water, thinking like a trout. There is creativity and imagination combined with precision and quality. "I take my time. I don't try to speed tie or anything like that. I like to tie them one at a time and then look at them, think about them, and go on to the next one," says Nourot. Successful fly-tying, like fly-fishing, requires the brain to be fully engaged, which doesn't leave much extra room for the mental clutter of daily tasks or routines. This particular craft can evoke pleasant memories of symphonic mountain streams, trout-filled pools reflecting the changing seasons, and furious fish-feeding frenzies on a pale morning dun hatch.

relaxation are close enough to touch from a single spot. There are only two chairs for furniture—one for Michael and one for the occasional guest. The place is more of a cabinet than a cabin. He says, "I like the size and scale a lot. It's a very small room but goes on forever. I actually feel like I'm sitting in a big, big room when I'm in there. For me, it's like a cave mentality or like a dog that has its favorite spot to rest." It is close, comfortable, familiar, reliable,

Even though Nourot has pursued retreat experiences in other places, this is the only phys-

The lunch crowd!

ical structure he has ever owned or really wanted for this purpose. After over fifteen years of continuously using The Executive Suite, he is firm in his own philosophy of retreat. "A retreat should be a private place where one can go to deal with their own thoughts. I think a retreat should be an essence of one's life—where one has been, where one is right now, and where one might want to be going. It is important because it gives you an introspection of who you are and what you are. We move way too fast in our society in the sense that we are not spending time examining ourselves and where we want to go."

Nourot also has some simple advice for others who are pondering their own place for personal solace: "Think small. Don't think about getting the baby grand piano in there, because then you'll have to get all of this other stuff in there too. Just think about getting yourself in there."

So what would Nourot do if late one night someone backed a pickup truck under the old camper and hauled it away? "Other than harm to my family, it's my worst nightmare. It's a very special place. Not only is all of my fishing gear there, but it has been home to thousands and thousands of moments of creativity, and thousands and thousands of memories are stored there. I would be devastated."

Having a place or a space, and getting yourself to it regularly seems to be the right place to start—and finish.

For Michael Nourot, The Executive Suite is a place of rest, refreshment and renewal, of new ideas and old ones, of old fish fooled and dreams of the next one. Amortized over fifteen-plus years, that's not a bad return for a home-built, tie-dyed hippie pickup camper acquired for $700 worth of dishes. A pretty good trade!

The goldfish pond is an additional retreat created by Nourot in a small slot of space behind the glassmaking studio. It is used by him and others for rest, reflection—and lunch.

125

Main Street Retreat

*God made the country,
and man made the town.*

WILLIAM COWPER

Though only 700 square feet in size, the traditional form, shape, and details of this building make it appear to be a "full-sized" house. The corrugated siding gives the appearance of shiplapped wood, but when the sun shines, so does Sandston's house.

WHEN MOST PEOPLE think of building a retreat, they are planning a way to get *out* of town. But for Stephanie Sandston it was about coming *to* town—a small town, but town nonetheless.

For a busy, often harried art director from Los Angeles who sometimes works thirty days in a row without a break, the little Montana town of Gallatin Gateway offers a stark contrast to the freeways, faceless people, and frequent smog of southern California. Designing sets for movies and television commercials is work that is pressure-filled and deadline-conscious, leaving little time for person-to-person connection. "When you are in a place like Los Angeles that has so much input all of the time, you start blanking out huge portions of the population," remarks Sandston. "You don't look people in the eye anymore. You don't notice if they say anything to you or not or if they smile, because

A reflective aluminum ceiling helps to give the living room/library a feeling of spaciousness.

Audrey Hall (left) and Stephanie Sandston relax for a moment of self-reflection.

you have tunnel vision. When I'm in Montana I'd feel hard pressed if somebody didn't wave when they passed by, whether they knew me or not. People pay a little more attention to the basics," she says. Life in Gallatin Gateway is at a different pace.

After spending time on a movie set on the banks of the nearby Gallatin River, Sandston felt the area tugging on her heart. "I fell in love. It was the most peaceful, relaxing place, where people were incredibly friendly. I just knew this was where I wanted to be."

She didn't start off thinking small or thinking town. Like so many who come to Big Sky Country, she had dreams of a much larger piece of property anchored by a more grandiose house. After rambling all over the Gallatin Valley looking at land and prices with her friend and architect Pete Stein, Sandston began to imagine

PHOTO © 1997 AUDREY HALL

herself as a "city" dweller. When three contiguous city lots became available right across the street from Stacy's Bar, Sandston made the purchase. The property, which totaled 120' x 150', was occupied by a trailer house and an old chicken coop. Then she struck a deal with Stein to design and build her retreat.

"I started out looking for a cabin or old farmhouse, but now I'm living in a town. It's kind of funky. It's not as if I am in a beautiful meadow. I'm on the main street, across from a bar."

Stein observes that it took a special person to locate her retreat in Gallatin Gateway. "To build in a small, ramshackle, unincorporated Montana town with no zoning, no town utilities, no speed limits or dog leash laws, it takes some guts, faith, and vision."

For Sandston, designing and building her retreat was a glorious experience. As a set designer for television commercials, she spends much of her time researching how other people live and then trying to recreate that experience on film. She designs buildings that last for thirty seconds on TV and then are torn down. For her, permanency was important. "To create something that was my own, that I wanted to be a lasting thing, was incredible. It is my first little place of my own."

For some, the decisions involved in creating a special personal space can be painstaking or sometimes even pain making, worrying about details, appearances, and having everything just right. However, because of the number of times she has interpreted the needs of others, Sandston had some pretty clear ideas about what she wanted for herself. "It was really clear to me and I wasn't nervous about the decisions I was making. This is the most fun I've had in

The compact kitchen, with cupboards built from a recycled chicken coop, acts as a display area for Sandston's collection of "found" objects.

A trayed bedroom ceiling, using attic space, makes a tiny space feel much larger.

years." Good advice for the retreat maker. Have fun, fully experience this set of moments, see the world through new eyes, and enjoy the ride. This will be good preparation for learning how to fully "retreat" when your finished dwelling is born.

Working together, Sandston and Stein made a number of "different" decisions about the design and about the building's finishes. In order to meet her construction budget, the entire building encompasses only 700 square feet—the size of some bedrooms in other Gallatin Valley vacation palaces. Two floors of 350 square feet each are stacked one on top of the other. "It looks like a birdhouse. It's a one-bedroom house that is two stories tall." Many would think the size entirely inadequate for a house. Not so for Sandston, who says, "The size is perfect. It is completely comfortable."

Her design criteria were actually quite simple. Besides meeting her tight budget, she says, "The house is designed around the fact that there has to be enough room for books, views to the mountains, and a place to cook good meals. Those are my basic necessities."

While giving it zest, Sandston also wanted it to fit into the surrounding streetscape—to fit into the town. Thus, the traditional farmhouse form but not completely traditional. "I wanted something warm and industrial," which are descriptive qualities not usually used in the same sentence. "I have trouble with little and charming, too charming, too much going on, especially given what I do professionally, where you are always putting more and more in because of how the camera sees it. It is great to have less."

The building is not sheathed in traditional farmhouse style—with the customary shiplap wood siding painted white—but rather with unpainted corrugated metal. Says Sandston, "It lights up when the sun hits it." Stein calls it the Farmer's Rocket.

The first-floor ceilings are aluminum sheets from a printing press, which create spatial inter-

est and softly reflect light down to the living space. Says Sandston, "It has a watery effect and creates a really great light." The kitchen cabinets are made from wood recycled from the old chicken coop out back, and the stair treads came from a building torn down at the local college. The upstairs flooring is seconds material that came from a local log-home builder. The ground floor is acid-washed concrete with hot-water heating embedded in the slab. Though Sandston admits that this heating approach was

Old fixtures, reflective walls, and a sloped ceiling enhance the quality of this tiny bathroom space.

A porch can be an important addition to any small retreat by protecting the front door from the weather, defining where the entry is, and inexpensively providing additional living space.

a bit more expensive, she has been pleased with her decision. "When you build a house in Montana, good, tight windows and good heating are not a mistake."

The interior decorations are a combination of old objects and art objects—but not too many. "I have collections. I come across too many objects to name in my everyday work—teapots, pottery, metal objects, things that I have collected on my journeys. It is a silly, fun, lighthearted collection of things—my favorite things."

The brightly colored Art Deco-style chairs came from a state surplus auction. "They originally were in a mental hospital. They were made in the twenties for the patients, and they all rock. How perfect is that for a retreat chair?"

When asked whether she had treated the corrugated metal siding to give it an "aged" effect,

Sandston replied that she had not. "It is what it is. Eventually the shine will come off and it will age itself. It will take care of itself in ten years. I want the house to be with me always and age on its own." In the final analysis, this building is respectful of its surrounding environment but not subservient to it. It fits in but with a personality all its own.

While it was under construction, Sandston's retreat was the talk of the town. Being right across the street from the Gallatin Gateway social center (spelled B A R) allowed the local architecture critics to create their own versions of why a young woman from California would want to build a corrugated metal birdhouse on the main street of town. Questions like "Is she going to paint it?" or "Is there another level going on it?" were discussed over beers or brandy Cokes.

But it was those same neighbors who were part of the attraction for Sandston. "The neighbors were as much of a draw as the place itself. One of my neighbors is an architect, one is a bookseller, and another is a brain biologist who works at the college. They are incredibly interesting people. Because I'm not working when I'm here, I have time to take part and get a little deeper into people's lives. I love the town I'm in."

The reality of her job and the necessity to commute from Los Angeles is not lost on Sandston, though the Bozeman airport is only a few miles away. "Reality means I have to keep working in L.A. Most people have to give up something to be here. For me, I have to be away from here so I can be here some of the time. The trade-off seems worth it, though. I'm ten times more at peace when I'm here. I'm a lot more focused without effort—to nature, to my own life, to other people's needs, and to the pace of life. Just being here brings my blood pressure down several notches."

Living within one's means is the primary advice Sandston has for aspiring retreat builders. "Design something you can afford. This retreat works for me because it takes care of the needs I have and I can afford it. When you can't afford it, it's painful and you don't take chances with your designs." Having enough control over your budget and design so that you can be assured of accomplishing your basic goals—while still having some room to be creative and have fun—is a good observation to put in one's retreat-planning notebook.

Sandston feels like she has already made some contribution to her adopted town by giving folks the opportunity to see a different perspective on things. She and Stein have noticed an increased interest in smaller buildings and in the design decisions they made that were out of the norm but smart, efficient, and a little more interesting. The questions have shifted from "Who is going to want a one-bedroom house?" to "How could I have a house like yours?" People seem willing to try something new.

"It is really interesting to get that kind of feedback," says Sandston. "It made me want to say, gee, everybody should have a little house that is helping a little town."

Stein sees what Sandston has done as an important message to other retreat builders. "Hopefully it will make a small contribution to stem the tide of the rampant subdivision of Montana's ranches and hinterlands. She is demonstrating that these small, rough towns with their history, character, and community are a viable place to build, fit in, and live."

PHOTO © 1997 AUDREY HALL

Care was taken by Sandston and Stein that the building they made would fit into the context and streetscape of the town where it was to live.

WINTER RETREATS

What a glorious time they must have in that wilderness, far from mankind and election day!

HENRY DAVID THOREAU

CARRYING 200 BUCKETS of water from beneath the icy crust of a frozen stream for the promise of a full-moon, wood-fired-hot-tub experience at 22 degrees below zero is enough to rid one's mind of other distractions. Before long, conversations shift and become full of meaning. The chaff blows away and the wheat remains. Almost as if by magic, new understandings emerge and self-discovery occurs. Feelings of exhilaration and the robustness of life are common at Fishhook Yurt in the Sawtooth Mountains of Idaho.

Just a few miles from the "I come here to be seen" scene of Sun Valley are magical wilderness places that can only be reached by foot, snowshoe, or cross-country ski. At least for now, many of those places are still inaccessible to snowmobiles and ATVs. These are the places Bob Jonas has chosen to roam, to know, and to work. After growing tired of being a ski instructor, he was called to

A standard horse trough, a wood-fired convection stove, plenty of dry wood, and 200 buckets of freezing stream water combine to create a refreshing outdoor bath that can be enjoyed in even the coldest weather.

the hills beyond the trams and took his passion for skiing into the backcountry—into the Sawtooths, Yellowstone, and the wilderness of Alaska.

Bob's calling to the wild places finally led him to pursue his livelihood as a backcountry outfitter. For over a decade Jonas has been leading small groups of ordinary people into the backcountry for unique retreat experiences by taking them on extended trips to relatively inaccessible places. There's no great fortune to be built by leading folk into the wilderness, but the riches for all involved are beyond one's usual units of measure. Days are gauged by the quality of experience. Time takes on a new dimension and is something to be savored, not saved.

What calls people from the warmth of their hearth or their office to the snowy wilderness where temperatures can easily reach the sub-teens in the nighttime hours? The motivations vary for every trekker. Some are looking to be suspended in the timeless nature of one perfect ski run in pristine powder snow without limits or

PHOTO © 1997 LAWSON DRINKARD

rules. Others fancy themselves as modern-day versions of Sir Richard Francis Burton, the nineteenth-century English adventurer who made a pilgrimage to Mecca.

Bob Jonas is not a television evangelist for the outdoors. His "ministry" sneaks up on folks, and before they know it they are under the spell of the experience he and Mother Nature provide. Leading people far away from phones, fax machines, and pagers into a world of frozen lakes, tall pines, and rugged mountains begins a process of clearing the mind and cleansing the spirit. Initially for most, the idea of retreat doesn't enter the picture. Opportunities for personal growth and profound learning experiences quietly wait to emerge as occasions arise.

As part of the whole experience, there are the retreats themselves—snow caves, wall tents, and yurts.

SNOW CAVES

"I was oriented toward the idea that people would be willing to trek into the winter back-country, the white wilderness, and sleep in snow caves, the most humble of shelters," explains Bob Jonas about starting his outfitting enterprise.

A snow cave is arguably one of the simplest and certainly one of the most temporary retreat structures that can be built. A firm snowbank, a shovel, and a tarp to cover the opening are the only tools and materials required. Usually used in lieu of carrying a tent on a high mountain trekking route, the snow cave is quiet, stable, and quite comfortable. In many ways it is the ultimate in the retreat experience.

Even with a retreat as elemental and temporary as a snow cave, the human spirit takes over with the desire to innovate, improve, and create a sense of place and community. Most winters Jonas leads

Bob Jonas cooking dinner in a snow cave in the Monolith Valley near Stanley, Idaho.

A snow cave will disappear with the spring thaw, but in the middle of winter it is a safe, secure retreat from howling winds and hoary frost.

a group across the Haute Route, a ten-day, seventy-mile trek across the Sawtooth peaks and passes. Invariably, as the days progress, the snow caves become more elaborate and expressive of their inhabitants. From simple shelters for cooking and sleeping, these habitats progress to frozen resort hotels with dining chambers, kitchens, boot shelves, and candleholders. The creative artist within each snow sculptor takes over for the sheer joy of making the space and enjoying it for what it is, if only for one day. The "building" lasts no longer than it takes for Sol to melt it down and recycle its power into the earth, but the experience lasts permanently in the minds of the creators.

WALL TENTS

For Bob Jonas, the wall tent especially evokes memories of his childhood. He believes that kind of recall is part of what makes a retreat place special. "I think all of us have a recollection that we jive on. It's very meaningful and brings up all

The brightly colored red and yellow nylon of the Bench Hut presents a warm contrast to the deep snow that almost buries it.

those images of delight, fun, and childhood. You know, the hunting camp and the wall tent after a day of rambling the hills. You come back to this cozy structure where there's a small sheepherder's stove kicking out the heat and the boys are all talking about the trail and passing a little stout juice. And then there's having some green meat

that's just been cooked. All of that's part of it. That's memory, recollection, wonderful things."

There is also a measure of history involved in the wall-tent retreat experience for Jonas. Every mining camp, early cow town, and backcountry hunting camp had wall tents.

One of Jonas's backcountry retreats is a wall tent called the Bench Hut. It is made of brightly colored yellow and red nylon and consists of a kitchen/dining area and a sleeping area with plywood bunk beds. Gasoline lanterns provide both light and warmth.

After a day of vigorous outdoor activity, attention is centered on tending the fire and creating a simple but elegant meal. Quick-fix recipes are avoided in favor of those that take thoughtful preparation, for it is in this shared activity that community is built. After dinner, given the lack of electronic accouterments, visiting is the only activity. As the day's events are recounted, façades peel away and the conversation becomes richer and more meaningful. Real dialogue begins to

occur. Sometimes the group will decide to share a reading or two. Especially appropriate is the Yukon poetry of Robert Service. Dan McGrew, Sam McGee, and Blasphemous Bill MacKie are familiar characters around the Sawtooth huts.

Outside, in addition to the roofed but open-air toilet that facilitates a beautiful view of the mountains, there is a wood-fired sauna that relaxes minds and muscles at the end of a long day of trekking. For those with a playful spirit and a strong heart, it is tradition at Bench Hut to emerge from the sauna and shock one's system by making a face-down snow angel before toweling off and jumping into waiting warm clothes!

In the middle of winter, snow stacks up around the walls of the tent, leaving only the translucent roof to glow like a giant striped caterpillar in the crisp night air. Jonas muses about the wall-tent retreat, "It's like wood smoke in the backcountry: it gets in your brain and permeates the consciousness at levels that make you love the whole experience."

The wall-tent kitchen serves as an area for swapping tales and building community.

A covered entry tunnel offers protection from the wind and snow at the
Tornak Hut near Ketchum, Idaho.

Bench Hut glows against the nighttime sky.

YURTS

When asked why he chose a Mongolian yurt structure for several of his retreat huts, Jonas replied, "It fascinated me to think it was tradition to the high plateaus of Asia, of Genghis Khan and company. And then it seemed close to the Native American tepee as a nomadic structure. So I looked at it and fell in love with it. I love the circular aspect, the idea of a very centered dome with light coming down. There's definitely something about yurt power."

In fact, the basic design of the yurt has not changed much in the 800 years since Genghis Kahn. Whereas the lightweight wooden lattice sides and wooden rafters were traditionally covered with layers of wool felt or skins, today's yurt construction starts with a circular wall frame of wooden lattice reinforced with a steel-cable tension ring. Wooden rafters that come together in the center are added and join a wooden hub, which is usually topped with a skylight. The entire frame is covered with a lightweight synthetic fabric that, depending on the use and climate, may contain layers of insulation.

Jonas's retreat yurts are twenty feet in diameter enclosing 314 square feet, or just about the

scope can immediately comprehend. This can result in feelings of peace, calm, relaxation—of centering your mind and spirit. A third factor is that the translucent skin and skylit dome create a soft natural light even during the waning moments of dusk. The light of a full moon is almost enough to read by, but certainly enough by which to dance and sing and make merry.

"Compared to a wall tent, a yurt is not as dark. It allows in more light. It seems to engender more life spirit," says Jonas.

There is also a beauty in the structural system itself. Alan Bair, owner of Pacific Yurts, Inc., calls it "elegance in the wilderness." He sees these structures as "a combination of ancient practicality and modern technology." According to Bair, his yurts have withstood 12-foot snowfalls and 98-mph winds at Mt. Hood in Oregon.

Jonas describes yurts as "earthquake proof. They're incredibly functional. The cable around the circumference on top of the lattice is the main structural element. It ties it all together. I can stand on the inside of the ring up there and my weight floats down and is essentially transferred through the many triangles of the lattice and is dispersed into the earth."

• • •

As Bob Jonas and his companion Sarah Michael prepared to embark on a twenty-seven-month expedition throughout the geographic regions of Alaska, which they call The Alaska Wilderness Odyssey, they became reflective. They would make the trek by sea kayak, on foot and skis. They planned to "winter" at small log cabins in the Alaskan bush where they would no doubt discover the extreme essence of a retreat experience.

Bob described a retreat as "some place to get away to undress your mind and to relax, and to even be meditative."

Sarah explained, "I learned after living in a Volkswagen camper for a year that small spaces can be a wonderful home and without the trappings and all the hassle of having too many pos-

The curved and convenient yurt kitchen has everything necessary for the preparation of simple and elegant dinners.

size of a modest-sized living room in an average American house. With bunk beds around the perimeter and a kitchen/dining area next to the woodstove, they will comfortably accommodate a dozen people.

The distinctive feelings one gets inside a yurt are probably promoted by a number of factors. For one, there is magic in the roundness. With no sharp corners, even a small yurt feels more spacious than similar square footage arranged in a rectangle. For another, there is a natural center that, on a subconscious level, one's inner gyro-

This 20-foot-diameter, 314-square-foot yurt can sleep fourteen people. Its lattice walls and wood rafters bound together with a top tension ring can withstand heavy snow and wind loads.

sessions. You don't have to worry about having the right pot. You make whatever pot you have work. And I see it as a very simplified lifestyle and as an opportunity to be creative."

Bob loves the idea of a small space because "it can restrain you from possessing much of anything. To me it is the antithesis of a materialistic culture. Most of our spaces are crammed with a lot of things that don't even have a two-year use record. What does that mean? It's just like your body: you overeat, you clog, you slow down, you're uncomfortable. You can make the same analogy with spatial things and living space.

"The small retreat has a lot of virtue. It forces you and in some ways empowers you to take another direction if you spend much time in them. I think we're scaling down a lot just going into this experience. And after living for two years in the wilderness, especially the cabin time, if we come out of that experience perfectly content—in fact, enriched—maybe we ought to look at what we've got and say, gee, what do we need other than a small retreat?"

A roofed, open-air toilet allows a clear view of the mountains beyond—and approaching visitors!

RETREATS IN WAITING

Until one is committed, there is hesitancy, the chance to draw back, always ineffectiveness, concerning all acts of initiative and creation. There is one elementary truth the ignorance of which kills countless ideas and splendid plans: that the moment one definitely commits oneself the Providence moves too. All sorts of things occur to help one that would never otherwise have occurred. A whole stream of events issue from the decision, raising in one's favor all manner of unforeseen incidents and meetings and material assistance which no man would have dreamed would have come his way. Whatever you can do or dream you can begin it. Boldness has genius, power and magic in it. Begin it now.

JOHANN WOLFGANG VON GOETHE

SOME YEARS AGO I heard a speech on the extraordinary potential of the human brain and the incredible untapped potential that resides in our unconscious mind. I never bothered to verify the statistics because the point wouldn't change even if the numbers were off a bit. The speaker said that the average human has fifty thousand thoughts per day, but only one to two thousand of those are conscious thoughts. The rest happen in our unconscious mind without us even knowing it. Just think about the extra potential if we captured even a small percentage of the other forty-eight thousand!

The speaker went on to point out that when we make a decision to move a thought, decision, or experience into our consciousness, we are frequently amazed at the number of times we notice something about it. For example, on any given day you might be passed on the road by one hundred green Ford pickup trucks and would never notice a single one. But let's say that you and your spouse decided at dinner last night that you were going to buy a green Ford pickup. The next day, and for weeks afterward, you would notice every one of them and be amazed by the number that were on the road now. Nothing changed but your mental perspective.

So, hoping that the possibility of a personal retreat will move from your unconscious to your conscious mind, I offer a few photographs and drawings of "retreats in waiting" to stimulate your thinking and whet your appetite. If you open your eyes and start to notice, you'll find hundreds more on your own, and my bet is that one of them will be well-suited for your particular purpose. Good luck and good hunting!

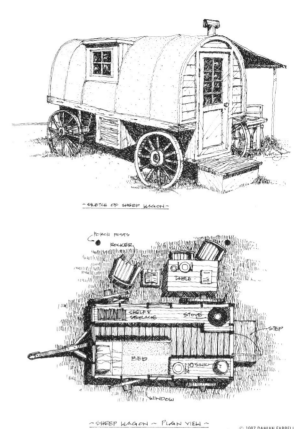

~ SKETCH OF SHEEP WAGON ~

PORCH POSTS
ROCKER
TABLE
SHELF &
STORAGE
STOVE
STEP
BED
SINK
WINDOW

~ SHEEP WAGON ~ PLAN VIEW ~

© 1997 DAMIAN FARRELL

~SILO~ CUT AWAY VIEW~

~SILO RETREAT~

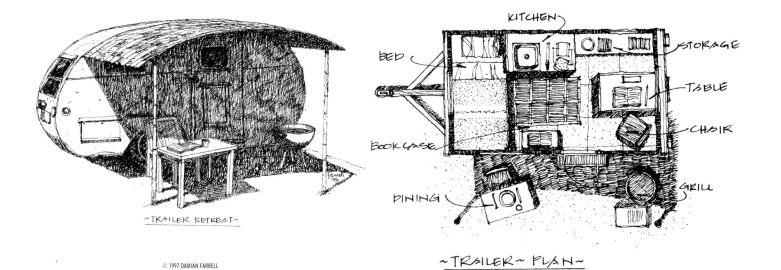

~TRAILER RETREAT~

© 1997 DAMIAN FARRELL

KITCHEN

BED

STORAGE

TABLE

CHAIR

BOOKCASE

DINING

GRILL

~TRAILER~ PLAN~

~WALL TENT~

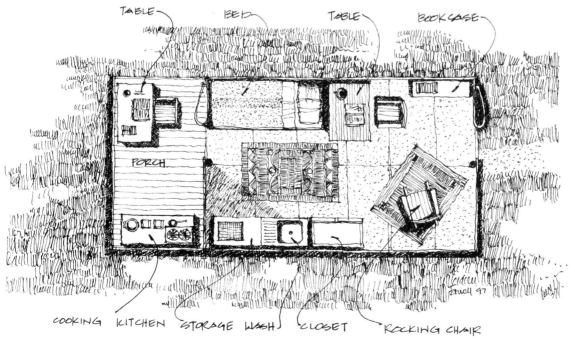

TABLE   BED   TABLE   BOOKCASE

PORCH

COOKING   KITCHEN   STORAGE   WASH   CLOSET   ROCKING CHAIR

~WALL TENT~ PLAN~

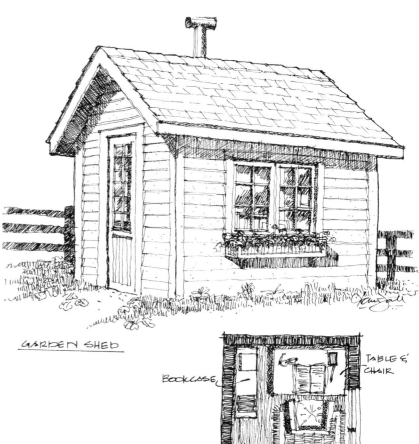

GARDEN SHED

BOOKCASE

TABLE & CHAIR

STOVE

© 1997 DAMIAN FARRELL

GARDEN SHED PLAN

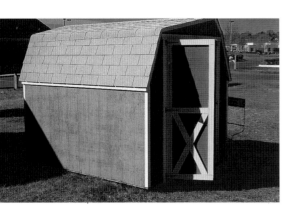

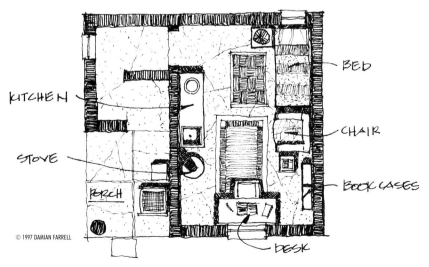

~BOMB SHELTER~

KITCHEN

STOVE

PORCH

© 1997 DAMIAN FARRELL

BED

CHAIR

BOOK CASES

DESK

~BOMB SHELTER~PLAN~

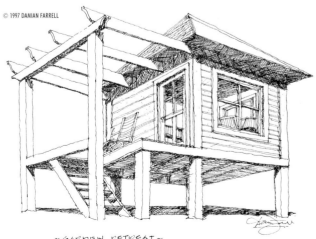

© 1997 DAMIAN FARRELL

~GARDEN RETREAT~

REFERENCES AND RESOURCES

RECOMMENDED READING

BOOKS

Berry, Wendell. *Harlan Hubbard—Life and Work.* Lexington: The University Press of Kentucky, 1990.
A wonderful description of Harlan and Anna Hubbard, a couple who lived their lives the way many imagine they would like their retreat experience to be.

Blue Evening Star. *Tipis & Yurts.* Asheville, North Carolina: Lark Books, 1995.
A historical and photographic essay on tipis and yurts with practical information to assist in building your own circular structure.

Bruchac, Joseph. *The Native American Sweat Lodge.* Freedom, California: The Crossing Press, 1993.
The history, meaning, and practical applications of Native American sweat lodges.

Bryner, Andy, and Dawna Markova, Ph.D. *An Unused Intelligence.* Berkeley, California: Conari Press, 1996.
A book that will assist in learning and practicing the retreat experience with physical exercises and gentle philosophical nudging to rediscover our inherent unused intelligence.

Burns, Max. *Cottage Water Systems.* Toronto: Cottage Life Books, 1993.
A complete guide to retreat water systems including water sources, pumps, plumbing, septic systems, outhouses and alternative toilets.

Cameron, Julia. *The Artist's Way.* New York: G. P. Putnam's Sons, 1992.
A self-taught course to discovering or rediscovering one's personal creativity.

Duncan, Dayton. *Miles from Nowhere.* New York: Viking Penguin, 1993.
A contemporary history of the last remaining frontiers in America. In addition to its historical and geographical interest, this book provides insights as to where and how some retreat in their everyday lives.

Easton, David. *The Rammed Earth House.* White River Junction, Vermont: Chelsea Green Publishing Company, 1996.
A practical guide to building a rammed-earth structure.

Edwards, Frank B., ed. *The Cottage Book.* Newburgh, Ontario: Hedgehog Productions, Inc., 1991.
A collection of helpful articles and practical advice in such diverse topics as furniture construction, bats, furniture refinishing and hauling a trailer safely.

Flood, Elizabeth Clair, and Peter Woloszynski. *Rocky Mountain Home.* Salt Lake City: Gibbs Smith, Publisher, 1996.
Narrative and photographs of a variety of homes that respect the landscape and surroundings in the Rocky Mountain West.

Hubbard, Harlan. *Payne Hollow—Life on the Fringe of Society.* Frankfort, Kentucky: Gnomon Press, 1974.
Hubbard's own description of living a simple yet rich life.

————. *Shantyboat—A River Way of Life.* Lexington: The University Press of Kentucky, 1977.
The chronicle of Harlan and Anna Hubbard's journey down the Ohio and Mississippi Rivers to New Orleans on a small and simple houseboat.

Hunt, W. Ben. *How to Build and Furnish a Log Cabin.* New York: Macmillan Publishing Company, 1974.
Originally published in 1939 and 1947, this book is a guide to building cabins and furniture with hand tools in the pioneer style.

Jaworski, Joseph. *Synchronicity.* San Francisco: Berrett-Koehler, 1996.
Jaworski's search for what was calling him forward gives the reader practical advice about discovering human possibilities.

Kylloe, Ralph. *Rustic Furniture Makers.* Salt Lake City: Gibbs Smith, Publisher, 1995.
Highlights a variety of styles and features sources for buying handmade rustic furniture, including chairs, settees, lamps, and more.

————. *Rustic Garden Architecture.* Salt Lake City: Gibbs Smith, Publisher, 1997.

A lavishly illustrated book on rustic garden furnishings ranging from benches and tables to gazebos and foot bridges.

———. *Rustic Traditions.* Salt Lake City: Gibbs Smith, Publisher, 1993.
A historical review of rustic furniture in America, as well as guidelines on what to look for when purchasing items from flea markets or antique dealers. Includes some sources for new rustic furnishings. Full color.

Laubin, Reginald and Gladys. *The Indian Tipi.* Norman: University of Oklahoma Press, 1957 (this printing, 1989).
According to Don Ellis, owner of White Buffalo Lodges and maker of tipis, this is the definitive guide to understanding the history and construction of the Native American tipi.

Manning, Richard. *A Good House.* New York: Penguin Books USA, 1993.
Manning's story of designing and constructing his own timber-framed house near Missoula is filled with practical and philosophical advice about everything from environmental issues to financing to alternative toilets.

McRaven, Charles. *Building with Stone.* Pownal, Vermont: Storey Communications, Inc., 1989.
An introduction to the philosophy, art, and craft of stone construction. Lots of practical information and pointers on selecting stone and on building dams, bridges, fireplaces, barns, and houses.

Nearing, Helen and Scott. *The Good Life.* New York: Schocken Books, 1989.
A treatise on the Nearing's philosophy and practice of rural homesteading.

Norris, Kathleen. *Dakota—A Spiritual Geography.* New York: Houghton Mifflin Company, 1993.
A contemplative book about appreciating people, place, and time. The chapter entitled "Getting to Hope" (Hope, South Dakota) is especially meaningful as one contemplates the place issues of a retreat.

Ramsey and Sleeper. *Architectural Graphic Standards,* 9th ed. New York: John Wiley and Sons, 1994.
A source book and standards guide for design and construction. Contains information on foundations, masonry construction, carpentry, fireplace design, moisture protection, site work and many other areas.

Steen, Steen and Bainbridge. *The Straw Bale House.* White River Junction, Vermont: Chelsea Green Publishing Company, 1994.
A complete overview of bale construction, including history, construction techniques, and design ideas.

Stiles, David. *Sheds—The Do-It-Yourself Guide for Backyard Builders.* Charlotte, Vermont: Camden House Publishing, 1994.
Design tips, construction techniques, and all kinds of sheds with drawings and photographs.

Taylor, Stephen. *Building Thoreau's Cabin.* Wainscott, New York: Pushcart Press, 1992.
Some philosophy and lots of practical guidance for building a simple personal retreat space at an affordable price.

Tillostson, Betty. *Skills for Simple Living.* Point Roberts, Washington: Hartley & Marks, Inc., 1991.
Practical ideas from outdoor clay ovens to simple solar hot water systems, and from gourd mandolins to bay leaf bug repellent.

Vickery, Robert L., Jr. *Sharing Architecture.* Charlottesville, Virginia: The University Press of Virginia, 1983.
A book for anyone who is interested in understanding the concepts and philosophy of architecture.

Walker, Lester. *Tiny Tiny Houses.* Woodstock, New York: The Overlook Press, 1987.
A compendium of floor plans and photos of forty tiny houses, none of which exceeds 325 square feet.

MAGAZINES

Home Power Magazine—The Hands-on Journal of Home-Made Power
P.O. Box 520
Ashland, Oregon 97520
Toll-free: (1-800) 707-6585
Fax: (916) 475-0941
A source for alternative energy.

Mother Earth News. New York: Sussex Publishers Inc.
A bimonthly magazine full of articles that range from bale houses, to single person hot tubs, to natural gardening tips as well as a source for purchasing retreat-related products and books.

Traditional Building. Brooklyn, New York: Historical Trends Corporation.
(Web: http://www.traditional-building.com)
A bimonthly magazine of articles, product information and sources for traditional building products.

Steve Aller
Boulder River Ranch
McLeod, Montana 59052
Phone: (406) 932-6406
*Custom steel cutouts, original ranch signs, and
cowboy cartoons.*

T. Baird Construction
Box 3
Big Timber, Montana 59011
Phone: (406) 932-6116
*Custom-built homes and retreats from used logs,
adapted structures, and salvaged materials. Also
new, if that's what you really want.*

Caravati's Inc.
104 East 2nd Street
Richmond, Virginia 23224
Phone: (804) 232-4175
*Salvaged materials from old buildings, including
stained glass, columns, doors, mantels, bathtubs,
iron gates, lighting, hardware, and old bricks.*

Cheap Joe's Art Stuff
374 Industrial Park Drive
Boone, North Carolina 28607
Toll-free: (1-800) 227-2788
Fax: (1-800) 257-0874
E-mail: cheapjoe@aol.com
Web: http://www.artscape.com/cheapjoe/
*Art supplies, materials, books, and a catalog that
promotes creativity, community, and the enjoyment
of life.*

Chuckwagon Outfitters
250 Avila Beach Drive
San Luis Obispo, California 93405
Toll-free: (1-800) 543-2359
Fax: (805) 595-7914
Cast-iron cookware, lanterns, books, and accessories.

Diane Cole Rustic Furniture
10 Cloninger Lane
Bozeman, Montana 59715
Phone: (406) 587-3373
One-of-a-kind custom willow and lodgepole furniture.

Cumberland General Store
#1 Hwy 68
Crossville, Tennessee 38555
Toll-free: (1-800) 334-4640
*Lamps, lanterns, fireplace accessories, blacksmith's
tools, windmills, hand pumps, porch swings, violin
kits, quilting frames, cider presses, country kitchen
utensils, and just about everything else.*

Damian Farrell Design Group
359 Metty Drive, Suite #3
Ann Arbor, Michigan 48103
Phone: (313) 998-1330
Fax: (313) 998-1340
Custom-designed residences and retreats.

Jon Golden
Box G
Charlottesville, Virginia 22903
Phone: (804) 971-8100
*Stock, people, portrait, location, industrial,
commercial, and wildlife photography.*

Audrey S. Hall, Photographer
121 North Yellowstone
Livingston, Montana 59047
Phone: (406) 222-2450
Photographs of your retreat or for your brochure.

Lehman's Non-Electric Catalog
P.O. Box 41
Kidron, Ohio 44636
Phone: (303) 857-5757
Fax: (303) 857-5785
*Nonelectric lighting, nonelectric appliances, cookstoves,
woodstoves, cast-iron cookware, and composting toilets.*

Montana Indian Contemporary Arts
Tyler Medicine Horse
P.O. Box 1674
Bozeman, Montana 59715
Phone: (406) 586-1441
Fax: (406) 586-0178
Referral agency for artists.

Montana Canvas Company
P.O. Box 390
Belgrade, Montana 59714
Phone: (406) 388-1225
Toll-free: (1-800) 235-6518
Fax: (406) 388-1039
*Source for wall tents, tent stoves, toilet tents, and
horse-packing gear.*

Montana Wagons
Box 1
McLeod, Montana 59052
Phone: (406) 932-4350
One-of-a-kind sheep wagon renovations, handcrafted into the retreat type and style of your choice.

Nourot Glass Studio
675 East H Street
Benicia, California 94510
Phone: (707) 745-1463
Fax: (707) 745-2181
Contemporary handblown glass.

Pacific Yurts, Inc.
77456 Highway 99 South
Cottage Grove, Oregon 97424
Phone: (541) 942-9435
Fax: (541) 942-0508
Web: http://www.yurts.com
A builder and supplier of yurts and accessories that range from 12' to 30' in diameter.

Real Goods
Toll-free: (1-800) 762-7325—telephone sales
Toll-free: (1-800) 919-2400—technical products
Fax: (707) 468-9394
Web: http://www.realgoods.com
E-mail: realgood@realgoods.com
Renewable energy products, sustainable lifestyle products, recycled products, including woodstoves, recycled paper products, hemp clothing, composting toilets.

Simpson Gallagher Gallery
1115 - 13th Street
Cody, Wyoming 82414
Phone: (307) 587-4022
Fax: (307) 587-5370
Western paintings, prints, sculpture and other items of delight and culture for your retreat.

Stokes of England
4085 Keswick Road
Keswick, VA 22947
Phone: (804) 295-1623
Web: www.archiron.com
Traditional blacksmiths and architectural ironwork consultants. If it can be forged from iron, you can get it made here.

Sun Valley Trekking
Bob Jonas
P.O. Box 2200
Sun Valley, Idaho 83353
Phone/fax: (208) 788-9585
Backcountry skiing and trekking adventures in Idaho, Wyoming, Montana, and Alaska.

Marc Taggart
831 Canyon Avenue
Cody, Wyoming 82414
Phone: (307) 587-9382
Dealer for original and reproduction Thomas Molesworth furniture.

Whispering Pines
P.O. Box 382
39 Edwards Street
Sparkill, New York 10976
Toll-free: (1-800) 836-4662
Fax: (914) 359-0717
Interior "things" for your retreat—furniture, decorations, books, and clothing.

White Buffalo Lodges
Don Ellis
P.O. Box 1382
Livingston, Montana 59047
Phone: (406) 222-7390
Fax: (406) 222-5725
Web: http://www.avicom.net/whitebuffalo
Producer of authentically designed Sioux, Crow, Cheyenne, and Blackfeet style tipis that range from 9' to 24' in diameter.

Wyoming Outdoor Industries, Inc.
1231 - 13th Street
Cody, Wyoming 82414
Phone: (307) 527-6449
Toll-free: (1-800) 725-6853
Fax: (307) 527-7508
Source for wall tents, woodstoves, toilet tents, shower tents, collapsible commodes, lanterns, cooking gear and horse-packing supplies.